Prix Fixe: Made in the USA by a Filipino

Hi Judy!
Happy Birthday to
you! Thank you for
the peppart! The book and
Enjoy the
recipes!
MABUHAY!

Prix Fixe: Made in the USA by a Filipino

Memoirs and Recipes of the Traveling Chef

ROMMEL MENDOZA

ISBN: 1542708303
ISBN 13: 9781542708302

The greatest gift a person can ever receive is life; for this I thank God, and our Savior Jesus Christ.
To my parents, I say thank you. Dad, your courage is unsurpassed, and little did I
know the many moves we made while you were in the US Army was a gift.
Mom, you will always be "the General", a born leader. By the way, Mom, the spankings you gave us
when we were young never hurt....we faked the crying, and laughed after you walked away.
To my wife, Eva....Thank you for allowing me to continue to dream while keeping me grounded. You
are the coconut on the cream pie, the strawberries on the cheese-cake, the mango in the gelato, etc.
You make my life taste so much better! And oh, I will continue to rock out to old-school jams!

Contents

Foreword

Rommel and I were traveling to Long Island on one of his first trips with Thompson Hospitality. The airplane was a roller coaster as we got ready to land, with bumps and sideways twists like I'd never felt before. Out of the corner of my eye, I remember seeing Rommel with his face pressed to the window looking out in wonder. Next thing I knew, he's in my face, very casually and calmly telling me that we were about to land sideways because he just saw the tail of the airplane from row 5 way up in the front. At that point, I knew that Rommel would be able to handle any situation he faced and would be someone who's fun to hang around with.

We traveled together a lot in the beginning. It always amazed me that after fourteen hours of hard work in a kitchen, he still had the energy and desire to find great local places where chefs were creating tremendous food. He's the first person I ever saw takes a picture of- *everything*, except what I needed. Rommel's focus is on food, creativity, and experimentation. What I needed, on the other hand, were pictures that proved an event was a success with quantitative evidence of customers, sales, business. His brain understands how important all that is, but it isn't how he judges success. Great food that makes people happy is success for Rommel.

Rommel has a lot of great stories to share. They are all true. He probably has a picture to prove each one.

I hope you enjoy this book, his collection of family, food, and culture with some humor thrown in, as much as I have enjoyed working with him. He has recently relocated to the west coast, where the culinary world is a melting pot of diversity. I am looking forward to seeing how these new opportunities and experiences influence his palette. I am a willing test subject if something needs to be sampled and taste tested, including great pickles. Speaking of which, I think he owes me a few jars!

– Stephen Pierce, Vice President of Retail Development, Thompson Hospitality

Preface

Let's see here, it is 3:00 a.m. on the eve of my birthday. What am I doing up? Well, I guess turning a year older may be the reason for my inability to sleep, but I think it is because of visions running through my head: wanting to open a restaurant, wanting to purchase a food truck, thinking of new recipes, getting older, there are so many things! But this morning, for some reason, I had a vision of wanting a book published; not just any ordinary book, but a memoir. In the past, though, I have always wanted to put a book of my recipes together as well. For those of you who may not know, which is more than likely many of you, I love to cook! It is in my *"sangre"* (Spanish for *blood*. I can still hear Señor Pappas from tenth- and eleventh-grade Spanish class saying that word. He would say it with such feeling.). Cooking is my passion. But do people really understand what passion means? From my point of view, passion comes from the heart and not just the mind. In other words, do something not because you have to do it, but because you want to do it. That is how I feel about cooking. So I figured why not put the two together.

In this book, you will read about events that have happened in my life. Also noteworthy, are events that occurred in my life while living overseas as well as present-day Virginia. I have traveled to many places in my short but eventful life span and have definitely experienced many things.

Before I get the show started here, one important thing I would like to say is that all the events and people mentioned in this book are not intended to poke fun at or ruin the character of anyone. What I am here to do is…well, just to put a smile on your face and say, "Yeah, I have done that before," or have you reminisce about the good times. I can see you smiling already. The events are all true; so just sit back, relax, and enjoy reading: *Prix Fixe: "Made in the USA by a Filipino" Memoirs and Recipes of the Traveling Chef.*

One

COCKTAILS
INTRODUCTION

I would like to thank you for giving me your time and choosing to read my book. You may say to yourself, "Wow, a chef and now an author!" Believe me, I am far from being an author. A chef, yes. In my opinion, anyone who has the passion to cook is a chef at heart. If you cook for your kids and they love it, they will think of you as their chef. If you cook for your significant other and he or she doesn't complain about the cuisine you prepared, then cooking is in you. When you are cooking for a group of people in a kitchen and you have kitchen help; guess what, you are a chef to them. *Merriam-Webster* dictionary's simple definition states, "A professional cook who is usually in charge of a kitchen in a restaurant or dining facility; a person who prepares food to eat." My definition of a *chef*...I am just a glorified dishwasher!

In this book, you will be introduced to Filipino cuisine; cuisine I have learned from my mother. She is the best chef (she is really a twice retired nurse of over forty years) who I know when it comes to Filipino cuisine. She is my biggest supporter but also my biggest critic. When it comes to my cooking of these authentic Filipino dishes, she will always have something to say about it. "There is too much salt" or "There is not enough vegetables" or "Why did you add that?"; I have heard all the criticism that any food critic can give a chef. But guess what, she always finishes with a compliment on every dish I have made for her. I think it is her way of saying, "I have taught him well."

Other than Filipino cuisine, I will share with you Filipino fusion recipes that I have put together while experimenting in the kitchen, cooking for guests, or just having fun with food. Last but not least, I will share refreshing and healthy smoothie recipes that I offered while operating my very own smoothie and deli shop years ago. Why did I write this book, you may ask. There are many cookbooks out there with interesting stories and recipes, ingredients that you may or may not have heard of, and recipes that sound and look amazing; but this book is different. I am a Filipino who was born in the motherland, raised by two hard-working and loving Filipino parents who were born and raised in the

Philippines. I want the world to know the basic Filipino cuisine and that it can be integrated with Old and New World recipes. Filipinos are here to stay, and our cuisine will soon be showcased worldwide! This is my story….

Where It All Started

Veterans Hospital, located in Quezon City, Philippines, is where I was born. My parents welcomed me, their second son, into the world on August 24, 1970, and gave me the name Rommel Allen Diaz Mendoza. I was a bouncing seven pounds, eleven ounces, and from seeing old pictures of myself, I already had a full head of hair! I hope that I don't lose it early in life. I am the younger of two boys who are part of this Mendoza family. I don't really understand why my parents stopped having children after me. Maybe they just didn't want any more. But you know what, I think because my head was so damn big when I was a baby, my mother probably swore never to endure again all the pain and crying when she was having me. Sorry, Mom. And no, my head isn't that big anymore. It goes well with the rest of my body.

My Name Is Rommel Allen Diaz Mendoza

Before I go on, let me first explain my full name: Rommel Allen Diaz Mendoza. *Rommel* is pronounced "Rome," like the city in Italy, and "*Mel*" as in, well, like "Mel's Diner." Easy enough, right? My first name is actually German. The name comes from the famous German officer General Erwin Rommel. I could give you the history of this famous general, but come on, this is not a history book. I can here you saying it! Now my last name *Mendoza* originates from Spain. Again, this is not a history book, but Spain ruled the Philippine islands for over three hundred years. I am just wondering which Señor Mendoza flirted with a Filipino woman and eventually won her heart. Maybe it was just one drunken, "debaucherous" night for good old Juan Mendoza looking for some tail! The surname *Mendoza* actually originates from the Basque region of Spain. The name means "cold mountain," derived from the Basque word *mendi* ("mountain") and *hotz* ("cold") and definite article "*a*." Hence *Mendoza* being *mendi+hotza*.

Allen is a name of European origin. The name is of English, Scottish, and Irish origin and means "fair" or "handsome." Hey, I like the sound of that! Lastly, *Diaz* is my mother's maiden name, and again it is of Spanish origin. To summarize, I have a German first name, two Spanish last names, and a European middle name. This is my full name, but guess what, I am a full-blooded Filipino! Hmmm…I am just wondering what party supplies my parents were enjoying when they were thinking of my name.

Orange Sunrise
Yield: 2-3 Servings

Ingredients:

2 c. oranges, fresh, peeled, cleaned
½ c. strawberry, cleaned, halved
10 ice cubes
1 c. orange juice
½ c. heavy cream
1 tbsp. strawberry jam
2 tbsp.honey

Procedure:

1. Wash and clean all fruits.
2. Place all ingredients in a blender. Cover.
3. Blend until smooth.
4. Make it your own. Add more fruits, substitute the heavy cream with ice cream, etc…
5. Enjoy!

Shanghai Lumpia
Yield: 24 - 36 half pieces

Ingredients:

2 lb. ground beef (80/20)
1 lb. ground Pork
1 c. onion, small dice
1 c. carrots, shredded
1 can water chestnuts, small dice
2 eggs, uncooked (minus shell)
1/2 c. soy sauce
2 tbsp. garlic powder
1 tbsp. kosher salt
1 tbsp. ground black pepper
1 tsp. dry basil
1 2 packs *lumpia wrapper (found in local Asian store)
1 plastic gallon bag
1 nonstick spray

*Make sure you purchase lumpia wrappers and not egg roll wrappers. Egg roll wrappers are traditionally thicker and wider than lumpia wrappers. Lumpia wrappers are made from rice paper or wheat flour, corn starch, and no egg.

Procedure: Mixture

1. In a large bowl, place mix ground beef, ground pork, onion, carrots, and water chestnuts together. Once mixed, form a well in the middle of the bowl.
2. Place 1 uncooked egg, soy sauce, garlic powder, kosher salt, ground black pepper, and dry basil in the well. Carefully break egg yolk and thoroughly mix all ingredients together.
3. Cover bowl with plastic wrap and place in refrigerator for 23 hours. I usually allow the filling to sit in the refrigerator overnight to fully marinate the ground meat with the added ingredients. Take lumpia wrapper out of freezer and place in refrigerator to allow to thaw.

Procedure: Rolling Lumpia

1. Take filling out of refrigerator. Allow to sit on counter at room temperature. During this time, take out lumpia wrapper from refrigerator and allow to sit in room temperature.

2. Liberally spray inside of gallon bag with nonstick spray.
3. Cut a piece off one bottom corner of the plastic gallon bag. The bigger the cut, the thicker the circumference of the end product will be. I usually cut a half inch off the corner.
4. Separate lumpia wrapper and place 57 wrappers on a clean work surface.
5. Place egg #2 in a bowl with a tablespoon of water. Create an egg wash. This will be used to close the wrapper.
6. Place filling in plastic bag and carefully squeeze out all the air. Filling should be at the tip of the opening that was created in the corner.
7. Similar to a cake piping bag, you will now use the plastic bag to pipe your lumpia filling.
8. Starting from one end of the wrapper, 1/4th from the bottom of each wrapper, slowly/carefully pipe the filling from one end of the wrapper to the other. Continue to do this until all 5–7 wrappers that were laid out have the filling on it.
9. Grab the bottom of the wrapper and carefully pull over filling and tuck underneath. Using the palms of your hands, roll filling leaving 1/2 inch of wrapper exposed.
10. Using a pastry brush, brush end of wrapper with egg wash. Finish rolling to close.
11. Line baking sheet with parchment paper and place finished raw lumpia on top.
12. Continue this process until all filling has been used.
13. Place unused wrapper back in original plastic wrap, fold, seal with tape, and place in a plastic gallon bag. Place back in freezer for later use.
14. Once all raw lumpia is on baking sheet, place in freezer overnight. This allows for the raw lumpia to properly seal so it does not open during the cooking process.

Cooking Process

1. Take frozen raw lumpia out of freezer. Carefully pull apart each raw lumpia due to it adhering to one another during the freezing process. Gently tap and pull apart if needed.
2. Place raw lumpia on cutting board and cut in half. Set cut raw lumpia to the side.
3. Using a medium stockpot, heat three cups of vegetable oil to 325 degrees. If you do not have a food thermometer, drop a pinch of flour into hot oil. If flour starts to sizzle in oil, oil is ready.
4. Place one end of cut raw lumpia in hot oil and carefully place the other end away from you. Continue to place raw lumpia in hot oil, making sure to leave enough room for lumpia to cook freely in hot oil.
5. Cook lumpia until wrapper is golden brown, about 35 minutes. If thicker raw lumpia is made, cooking process will be 57 minutes.
6. Place cooked lumpia on metal strainer. This will allow excess oil to drain from the finished product. If there's no strainer, place on flat container lined with paper towel.
7. Serve with garlic-lemon-infused soy sauce, sweet chili sauce, or by itself. Eat and Enjoy!

TWO

Brief History of the Philippines

Rather than writing about the history of the Philippines, I will only write a brief synopsis of this jewel of a nation regarding its archipelago, climate, language, and historical events. What I would like to elaborate more is why Filipinos are special. This will be answered by an essay by Pastor Ed Lapiz that I included.

The Philippine Islands is an archipelago consisting of 7,107 islands; the main island groups are Luzon, Visayas, and Mindanao, and the capital is Manila. Along with its many islands, the Philippines has many dialects, five hundred in total. The eight main dialects are Tagalog, Cebuano, Ilocano, Hiligaynon, Bicol, Waray, Pampango, and Pangasinense. Tagalog is considered the national language.

There are three distinct seasons in the Philippines. The rainy season (June through September), the cool and dry season (October through February), and the hot and humid season (March through May). Typhoons, similar to hurricanes in Florida, occur from June to September.

The Filipino People

It is a known fact that we have come from islands that were in close proximity to the Philippine Islands. If you look into the history of the most remote and oldest tribes, you will find that Filipinos originated from negro background similar to the Australians. Since many islands and countries were in close proximity to the Philippines, many neighboring peoples such as the Chinese and the Australians migrated to the island. Along with Spanish and European settlement, mainland Asia and Japan migrations to the islands started to change the face of the Philippine people, giving it a more diverse look. With these migration groups from Asia and the Pacific island group, the negro tribes that were once predominant on the island soon became deluded. Filipinos soon adapted the Asian as well as European identity.

Other than the short history lesson of where Filipinos may have come from, I feel the best way to illustrate who Filipino people are is best described by Filipino pastor Ed Lapiz.

Why Filipinos Are Special
by Pastor Ed Lapiz

Filipinos are brown. Their color is in the center of human racial strains. This point is not an attempt at racism, but just for many Filipinos to realize that our color should not be a source of or reason for inferiority complex. While we pine for a fair complexion, the others are religiously tanning themselves, whenever they could, under the sun or some artificial light, just to approximate the Filipino complexion.

Filipinos are a touching people. We have lots of love and are not afraid to show it. We almost inevitably create human chains with our perennial "akbay" (putting an arm around another shoulder), "hawak" (hold), "yakap" (embrace), "himas" (caressing stroke), "kalabit" (touch with the tip of the finger), "kalong" (sitting on someone else's lap), etc. We are always reaching out, always seeking interconnection.

Filipinos are linguists. Put a Filipino in any city, any town around the world. Give him a few months or even weeks and he will speak the local language there. Filipinos are adept at learning and speaking languages. In fact, it is not uncommon for Filipinos to speak at least three: his dialect, Filipino, and English. Of course, a lot speak an added language, be it Chinese, Spanish or, if he works abroad, the language of his host country. In addition, Tagalog is not "sexist." While many "conscious" and "enlightened" people of today are just by now striving to be "politically correct" with their language and, in the process, bend to absurd depths in coining "gender sensitive" words, Tagalog has, since time immemorial, evolved gender-neutral words like "asawa" (husband or wife), "anak" (son or daughter), "magulang" (father or mother), "kapatid" (brother or sister), "biyenan" (father-in-law or mother-in-law), "manugang" (son or daughter-in-law), "bayani" (hero or heroine), etc. Our languages and dialects are advanced and, indeed, sophisticated! It is no small wonder that Jose Rizal, the quintessential Filipino, spoke some twenty-two languages!

Filipinos are groupists. We love human interaction and company. We always surround ourselves with people and we hover over them, too. According to Dr. Patricia Licuanan, a psychologist from Ateneo and Miriam College, an average Filipino would have and know at least 300 relatives. At work, we live "bayanihan" (mutual help); at play, we want a "kalaro" (playmate) more than "laruan" (toy). At socials, our invitations are open and it is more common even for guests to invite and bring in other guests. In transit, we do not want to be separated from our group. So what do we do when there is no more space in a vehicle? "Kalung-kalong!" (Sit on one another). No one would ever suggest splitting a group and waiting for another vehicle with more space!

Filipinos are weavers. One look at our baskets, mats, clothes, and other crafts will reveal the skill of the Filipino weaver and his inclination to weaving. This art is a metaphor of the Filipino trait. We are social weavers. We weave theirs into ours that we all become parts of one another. We place a lot of premium on "pakikisama" (getting along) and "pakikipagkapwa" (relating). Two of the worst labels, "walang pakikipagkapwa" (inability to relate), will be avoided by the Filipino at almost any cost. We love to blend and harmonize with people, we like to include them in our "tribe," in our "family"—and we like to be included in other people's families, too. Therefore we call our friend's mother "nanay" or mommy; we call a friend's sister "ate" (eldest sister), and so on. We even call strangers "tita (aunt) or "tito" (uncle), "tatang" (grandfather), etc. So extensive is our social openness and interrelations that we have specific title for extended relations like "hipag" (sister-in-law's spouse), "balae" (child-in-law's parents), "inaanak" (godchild), "ninong/ninang" (godparents), "kinakapatid" (godparent's child), etc. In addition, we have the profound "ka" institution, loosely translated as "equal to the same kind" as in "kasama" (of the same company), "kaisa" (of the same cause), "kapanalig" (of the same belief), etc. In our social fiber, we treat other people as co-equals. Filipinos, because of their social "weaving" traditions, make for excellent team workers.

Filipinos are adventurers. We have a tradition of separation. Our myths and legends speak of heroes and heroines, who almost always get separated from their families and loved ones and are taken by circumstances to far-away lands where they find wealth or power. Our Spanish colonial history is filled with separations caused by the reduction (hamleting), and the forced migration to build towns, churches, fortresses or galleons. American occupation enlarged the space of Filipino wandering, including America, and there are documented evidences of Filipino presence in America as far back as 1587. Now, Filipinos compose the world's largest population of overseas workers, populating and sometimes "threshing" major capitals, minor towns and even remote villages around the world. Filipino adventurism has made us today's citizens of the world, bringing the "bagoong" (salty shrimp paste), "pansit" (sautéed noodles), "siopao" (meat-filled dough), "kare-kare" (peanut-flavored dish), "dinuguan" (innards cooked in pork blood), "balut" (unhatched duck egg), and "adobo" (meat vinaigrette), including the "tabo" (ladle) and "tsinelas" (slippers) all over the world.

Filipinos are excellent at adjustments and improvisation. Filipinos manage to recreate their home, or to feel at home anywhere.

Filipinos have "pakiramdam" (deep feeling/discernment). We know how to feel what others feel; sometimes even anticipate what they will feel. Being "manhid" (dense) is one of the worst labels anyone could get and will therefore, avoid at all cost. We know when a guest is hungry though the insistence on being full is assured. We can tell if people are lovers even if they are miles apart. We know if a person is offended though he may purposely smile. We know because we feel. In our "pakikipagkapwa" (relating), we get not only to wear another man's shoe but also his heart. We have a superbly developed and honored gift of discernment, making us excellent leaders, counselors, and go-betweens.

Filipinos are very spiritual. We are transcendent. We transcend the physical world, see the unseen and hear the unheard. We have a deep sense of "kaba" (premonition) and "kutob" (hunch). A Filipino wife will instinctively feel her husband or child is going astray, whether or not telltale signs present themselves. Filipino spirituality makes him invoke Divine presence or intervention at nearly every bend of his journey. Rightly or wrongly, Filipinos are almost always acknowledging, invoking or driving away spirits into and from their lives. Seemingly trivial or even incoherent events can take on spiritual significance and will be given such space or consideration. The Filipino has a sophisticated, developed "pakiramdam." The Filipino, though becoming more and more modern (hence, materialistic) is still very spiritual in essence. This inherent and deep spirituality makes the Filipino, once correctly Christianized, a major exponent of the faith.

Filipinos are timeless. Despite the nearly half-a-millennium encroachment of the western clock into our lives, Filipinos—unless on very formal or official functions—still measure time not with hours and minutes but with feeling. This style is ingrained deep in our psyche. Our time is diffused, not framed. Our appointments are defined by "umaga" (morning), "tanghali" (noon), "hapon" (afternoon) or "gabi" (evening). Our most exact time reference is probably "katanghaliang-tapat" (high noon), which still allows many minutes of leeway. That is how Filipino trysts and occasions are timed: there is really no definite time. A Filipino event has no clear-cut beginning nor ending. We have a fiesta, but there is "bisperas" (eve), a day after the fiesta is still considered a good time to visit. The Filipino Christmas is not confined to December 25th; it somehow begins months before December and extends up to the first days of January. Filipinos say good-bye to guests first at the head of the stairs, then down to the "descamo" (landing), to the "entresuelo" (mezzanine), to the "pintuan" (doorway), to the "tarangkahan" (gate), and if the departing persons are to take public transportation, up to the bus stop or bus station. In a way, other people's tardiness and extended stays can really be annoying, but this peculiarity is the same charm of Filipinos who, being governed by timelessness, can show how to find more time to be nice, kind, and accommodating than his prompt and exact brothers elsewhere.

Filipinos are spaceless. As in the concept of time, the Filipino concept of space is not numerical. We will not usually express expanse of space with miles or kilometers but with feelings in how we say "malayo" (far) or "malapit" (near). Alongside with numberlessness, Filipino space is also boundless. Indigenous culture did not divide land into private lots but kept it open for all to partake of its abundance. The Filipino has avidly remained "spaceless" in many ways. The interior of the "bahay-kubo" (hut) can easily become receiving room, sleeping room, kitchen, dining room, chapel, wake parlor, etc. depending on the time of the day or the needs of the moment. The same is true with the "bahay na bato" (stone house). Space just flows into the next space that the divisions between the "sala," "caida," "comedor," or "vilada" may only be faintly suggested by overhead arches of filigree. In much the same way, Filipino concept of space can be so diffused that one's party may creep into and actually expropriate the street! A family business, like a sari-sari store or "talyer" may extend to the sidewalk and street. Provincial folks dry "palayan" (rice grain) on the highways! Religious groups of various persuasions habitually and matter-of-factly commandeer the streets for processions and parades. It is not uncommon to close a street to accommodate private functions. Filipinos eat, sleep, chat, socialize, quarrel, even urinate, nearly everywhere or just anywhere! "Spacelessness," in the face of modern, especially urban life, can be unlawful and may really be counter-productive. On the other hand, Filipino "spacelessness," when viewed from his context, is just another manifestation of his spiritually and communal values. Adapted well to today's context, which may mean unstoppable urbanization,

Filipino "spacelessness" may even be the answer and counter balance to humanity's greed, selfishness and isolation.

So what makes the Filipino special? We are brown, spiritual, timeless, spaceless, linguists, groupists, weavers and adventurers. Seldom do all these profound qualities find personification in a people. Filipinos should allow—and should be allowed to contribute their special traits to the world-wide community of men and women—but first, we should know and like ourselves.

Best Ever Chicken Salad

Yield: 6–8 sandwiches

Ingredients

3 lb. chicken breast
1 bay leaf
3 c. water
1 tbsp. garlic, fresh, minced
1/2 c. red onion, grilled then small dice
1/4 c. yellow onion, small dice
1/4 c. green onion, small chopped
1 Granny Smith apple, skin off, cored, small diced
2 tbsp. cilantro, fresh, chopped fine
1 c. mayonnaise
1 tbsp. olive oil
2 tbsp. yellow mustard
2 tsp. black pepper
2 tsp. kosher salt
2 tsp. garlic powder
1 tsp. brown sugar
1/2 tsp. dry basil

Procedure

1. Turn on stove to medium-high heat. Place 1.5 pounds of chicken breast in small pot; add water and bay leaf. Cook for about 20 minutes or until chicken is cooked through. Once cooked, place on flat container and let cool. Keep chicken broth for later use.
2. Turn on the grill. Combine 1 teaspoon of black pepper, kosher salt, and garlic powder in a bowl; mix well. Season other 1.5 pounds of chicken breast on both sides. Place in flat container at room temperature until grill is hot.
3. Once hot, carefully place raw chicken breast on top of grill. Cook for about 10–15 minutes or until juices run clear and chicken is cooked through. Place red onion on grill and cook on both sides. Once cooked, place grilled chicken and red onion on same flat container as poached chicken; let cool.
4. Once cooled, hand shred both types of chicken and place in large bowl.
5. Add garlic, all onions, Granny Smith apple, and fresh chopped cilantro. Mix Well.

6. Add olive oil, mayonnaise, yellow mustard, black pepper, kosher salt, brown sugar, dry basil, and garlic powder. Mix until well incorporated.
7. Add more olive oil or mayo if too dry.
8. Place a heaping mound of chicken salad on toasted choice of bread, spread over crackers or use as a dip for your favorite veggies. Taste, share, and enjoy!

Chicken Adobo

Yield: 6–8 servings

Ingredients

6–8 chicken thighs, drums, wings or breast (can be a mixture of pieces)
1 c. soy sauce
2/3 c. white distilled vinegar
1/4 c. pineapple juice
1/2 c. yellow onion, diced
1/4 c. garlic, fresh, chopped
1 tbsp. ground black pepper
2 tbsp. brown sugar
1 tsp. dry basil
1 tbsp. Mrs. Dash Spicy Seasoning Mix
2 bay leaves
1 tsp. whole black peppercorns
1 can pineapple chunks (save juice for marinade)

Directions

1. Drain pineapple from can and save the juice. Keep pineapples cool for later use.
2. Pour soy sauce, white vinegar, and pineapple juice in a bowl. Add onions, garlic, ground black pepper, brown sugar, and dry basil. Mix well.
3. Place chicken in a sealable container. Carefully pour marinade over chicken; mix well, making sure to coat each piece of chicken. Cover or seal and place in refrigerator. Marinate 4–6 hours; overnight is best.
4. After marinating, place chicken along with marinade in a big enough pot to hold contents. Add Mrs. Dash, bay leaves, and whole peppercorns. Cook on medium high until mixture begins to boil, about twenty minutes.
5. Once boiling, gently stir then turn heat down to medium. Add pineapples and cook for an additional 15–20 minutes.
6. Spray baking sheet with nonstick cooking spray. Heat oven to 350 degrees Fahrenheit.
7. Place chicken on baking sheet and place in the oven. Allow chicken to further cook and caramelize for about 10–15 minutes. Keep sauce warm.
8. Take cooked chicken out of oven, place over rice, and spoon sauce/pineapple chunks over chicken.
9. Enjoy

Chicken Lumpia Filling

Yield: 15–20 servings

Ingredients

2 lb. chicken thighs (boneless, skinless)
2 bay leaves
4 c. water
2 tbsp. vegetable oil
2 tbsp. garlic, minced
1 onion, medium, small dice
2 tbsp. black pepper
2 tbsp. garlic powder
1 tbsp. kosher salt
1 c. soy sauce
1 c. carrots, cleaned, halved lengthwise, cut on a bias, then sliced thin
1 c. green beans, ends cut, sliced on a 1-in. bias
1 c. celery with leaves, cleaned, halved lengthwise, sliced thin on a bias
1/2 head green cabbage, shredded
1 c. mung bean sprouts

Dipping Sauce

1 c. soy sauce
1/2 c. lemon juice
1 tsp. ground black pepper
1/2 tsp. dry basil

Procedure

1. Turn stove to medium-high heat. Place chicken and bay leaves in a medium stockpot; add water. Bring chicken to a boil then reduce to a simmer. Cook for 20–25 minutes or until chicken is fully cooked.
2. Discard bay leaves; place cooked chicken thighs in a bowl, set aside, let cool to room temperature. Place chicken cooled stock in a container; set aside for later use.
3. Once chicken has cooled, shred then set aside.
4. Place a medium-size pot on medium-high heat. Heat oil then add onions and garlic. Saute for three minutes or until garlic turns light brown and onions are translucent. Add carrots, green

beans, celery, 1/2 cup of soy sauce, 1 tablespoon of ground black pepper, 1 tablespoon of garlic powder. Mix well and saute for 5 minutes.

5. Add bean sprouts, shredded cabbage, remaining black pepper and garlic powder, cooked sliced chicken thighs, and 1/2 cup of soy sauce. Mix well, saute for another 3–5 minutes. MAKE SURE NOT TO OVERCOOK VEGETABLES! Turn off the stove and take off heat. Place vegetables in a shallow container to cool.

6. Pour reserved liquid with chicken stock; cool and place in refrigerator for later use.

7. Allow chicken and vegetable mixture to cool before rolling. (I usually place mixture in the refrigerator for at least 2–4 hours.)

Procedure: Rolling Lumpia

1. Take filling out of refrigerator; allow to sit on counter at room temperature. During this time, take out lumpia wrapper from refrigerator and place on counter in room temperature.

2. Separate lumpia wrapper and place 5–7 wrappers on a clean work surface; slightly turn it to form a diamond shape.

3. Place egg no. 2 in a bowl with a tablespoon of water; create an egg wash. This will be used to close the wrapper.

4. Using a tablespoon, spoon 2 tablespoons of the lumpia mixture about a third above the bottom point of the diamond.

5. Grab the bottom point of the wrapper and carefully pull over filling, and tuck underneath. Tuck the bottom point of the wrapper under the filling; roll the covered mixture tightly but carefully, making sure not to tear.

6. Fold over the right and left points of the wrapper to the center of the rolled wrapper; roll again.

7. Using a pastry brush, brush end of wrapper with egg wash. Finish rolling to close.

8. Line baking sheet with parchment paper and place finished uncooked lumpia with egg-washed side on the bottom.

9. Continue this process until all filling has been used.

10. Place unused wrapper back in original plastic wrap, fold, seal with tape, and place in a plastic gallon bag. Place back in refrigerator for later use.

11. Once all uncooked lumpia are on baking sheet, place in freezer overnight. This allows for the uncooked lumpia to properly seal so it does not open during the cooking process.

Cooking Process

1. Take frozen uncooked lumpia out of freezer. Carefully pull apart each uncooked lumpia due to it adhering to one another during the freezing process; gently tap and pull apart if needed.

2. Using a medium saute pan, heat 3 cups of vegetable oil to 325 degrees. If you do not have a food thermometer, drop a pinch of flour into hot oil. If flour starts to sizzle in oil, oil is ready.

3. Place one end of uncooked lumpia in hot oil and carefully place other end away from you. Continue to place lumpia in hot oil, making sure to leave enough room for lumpia to cook freely in hot oil.

4. Cook lumpia until wrapper is golden brown on one side; about 3–5 minutes. Using tongs, carefully turn over and cook for another 3–5 minutes or until golden brown.

5. Place cooked lumpia on metal strainer; this will allow excess oil to drain from finished product. If no strainer, place on paper-towel-lined flat container.

6. Continue to cook until complete. Add more oil, if needed, during the cooking process.

7. Serve with soy sauce and/or lemon dipping sauce.

8. Eat, share, and enjoy!

Island–Style Tomato Soup

Yield: 8–10 servings

Ingredients

5 lb. tomatoes, fresh, cleaned, quartered
1 garlic bulb, cleaned and separated
1 c. basil, fresh, chopped
2 tbsp. kosher salt
2 tbsp. black pepper
2 c. carrots, washed, cleaned, small dice
2 c. celery, washed, cleaned, small dice
2 c. yellow onion, small dice
2 c. ripened mango, deseeded, cleaned, small dice
2 tbsp. olive oil
2 diced tomato, 12 oz. can
3 tbsp. dried basil
2 tbsp. garlic powder
2 c. almond coconut milk
3 tbsp. brown sugar
kosher salt (to taste, if needed)

Procedure

1. Turn stove to medium-high heat. Place fresh tomatoes, garlic, 3/4 cup of fresh basil, kosher salt, and black pepper in a large stockpot. Cook until tomatoes have softened. Stir occasionally.
2. While tomatoes are cooking, using a large saute pan, heat olive oil. Add carrots, celery, yellow onion, and mango. Saute for 5–7 minutes. Add canned diced tomatoes and garlic powder. Saute for another 5–7 minutes until all vegetables have softened.
3. Add sautéed vegetable and tomato mixture to stockpot. Mix well. Turn heat down to medium. Using a hand blender, combine mixture together and puree.
4. Cut remaining basil in long, thin strips (chiffonade) and add to mixture; slowly stir.
5. Add dried basil, kosher salt, and garlic powder, almond coconut milk, and brown sugar; carefully stir.
6. Turn heat down to low and continue to cook for another 15–20 minutes; add more kosher salt if needed.
7. Serve hot with toasted garlic bread, fried plantains, banana chips, or by itself.
8. Taste, share, and enjoy!

Three

AMUSE-BOUCHE
MEMOIRS, THE PHILIPPINES

My Grandmother Canota and the Switch

An amusing story I would like to share happened to me when I was four years old. My older brother attended kindergarten at the time, so I played with my cousin who lived across the street while my brother was at school. For those of you who have never been to the Philippines, try sticking your head—well, maybe not your head, but your hand in a hot oven for a couple of minutes. That is how hot it can get in the Philippines during the summer. Anyway, this particular day was very hot, and my cousin and I wanted to go and play in the water at the riverbank. Even though the river was only a hundred yards away, our grandmother did not want us to go to the river and instructed us not to leave the yard. Now what do you think we did? As soon as my cousin reached the foot of the river, he jumped right in. He was quite excited about how cool the water was and screamed for me to jump in. I was looking down at him from the bridge and started making my way to one side in order to go down to the riverbank. Before I could even reach the side of the bridge, I saw a woman in an old dress. Both hands formed a fist, and she had a quick step in her walk even though she dragged her feet while walking. Did I mention that she had a switch as long as a yardstick in one of her hands? (Keep in mind that this was during the seventies, when good old-fashioned "whoopin" was still allowed. Plus, this was in the Philippines, where I am sure parents still open up that can of whoop ass if their children misbehave.) It was our grandmother! Now do you think I made it to the water? I started walking slowly toward her with my head down and my big lips sticking out. I was still a good thirty yards from her when the dams of my eyes opened up and tears started streaming down my face. I was crying my eyes out, for I knew I was going to get a switch beating that I never had before. Twenty yards, fifteen yards, ten yards, five; then, she was right there in front of me. I closed my eyes and clenched my butt cheeks and let out a loud cry.

My grandmother stopped and asked in our native tongue, "What's wrong with you? Why are you crying?"

Now when she uttered those words, the crying stopped a bit, and I was stunned. I looked at her with snot coming out of my nose, tears racing down my round face, and my big lips sticking out and said, "I don't know."

She then commanded me to go straight home and eat. "Okay" was the last word I said to her while she continued on her trek to whip some booty. I was about fifteen yards away when I slowly turned around and saw her grab my cousin out of the river, dragged him up on the road, and started switch whipping him like an unruly boy deserves. I felt sorry for my cousin, but then again, I was glad I didn't get a taste of that. The last comment I remembered saying in my native tongue, "I told you we should have never left the yard."

Saved by Dad

Another event that happened to me at a very young age in the Philippines is one I still remember like it happened yesterday. I was five years of age. It had rained substantially for two days straight, and when this happens, the town we lived in (Paombong, Bulacan, Philippines) would get flooded. My grandparents' yard was flooded, but since their house was on higher ground, the water did not go above the walkway that surrounded their house. During this time, I was out on the walkway on my little tricycle. My dad had warned me not to go too close to the edge since the water level was still high from the flood. I don't recall if I listened to my dad or not, but the next thing I remember is falling into the water! I started sinking fast, and I did not know how to swim. For some reason, my eyes were wide-open, and I was sinking toward the bottom. I'm sure they were open because to this day, I can still see myself going lower and lower to the bottom. It seemed like hours that I was going deeper into the water. Without even realizing I was drowning, my dad jumped in and grabbed me and pulled me to the top and set me on the walkway. I was coughing and crying at the same time. My dad just held me there for a bit and then told me everything was going to be fine. After over forty years, I still remember that day.

"You can kiss her there but not there..."

After leaving our beloved Germany (Heidelberg, Germany) after I graduated from high school in 1988, my entire family headed to the Philippines to visit family and friends before the big move back to the United States. My dad was still in the US Army during this time, and his next tour of duty was at the Pentagon. We had not been back to visit the Philippines as a family for quite some time, so this was the perfect time to spend the summer with old friends and with relatives in the motherland.

One particular steamy afternoon, my brother, Roland, and I were smoking cigarettes (we were both rebels, and cigarettes were part of our young lives during this time), talking and patiently waiting for time to go by as we sat under the mango tree at my lolo and lola's house. This is what we call our grandparents on my mother's side. The house was built on ten acres of land in a small town called Aringay in the province of La Union. There is not much to do in a small town, so we did what most young adults would do in a foreign country would do. We did absolutely nothing except watch cars go by, eat all day long, and smoke cigarettes (yes, I know, that is bad for you).

As my brother and I patiently waited for something to happen, our Lolo Felipe slowly walked around the corner, squatted, and joined us in our brotherhood. Our Lolo Felipe was ninety-five years old at this time. He moved slowly but was very active for his age. Tending to the garden, chopping down small branches, and taking afternoon naps were his favorite things to do. He was an educated man, a principal at the town elementary school, and was well-known among everyone who lived in Aringay. I guess he had just woken up from his nap and decided to join in our discussion.

"May I have a cigarette?" Lolo politely asked.

Roland quickly pulled one out of his pack, and I lit it as Lolo took one big inhale and slowly let the smoke escape his lungs.

"You know, when I was your age, I had a lot of girlfriends. Some were nice and others were even nicer." He smiled after he exhaled the smoke from his lungs. "But when I met your Lola Alberta, I fell in love. She made me smile all the time. There was something about her that made me know that she would be my wife."

My lolo had touched my heart.

He continued, "I know your Lola Alberta writes you letters, and she very much loves receiving letters from the two of you. It makes her smile to know that her grandchildren are doing well in life. So please keep writing her. It makes her very happy. I also know that she lectures that you should not have any girlfriends, concentrate on your studies [school], get a good job, and don't get married early. I agree with your Lola Alberta about all that she says, but there are things in this world that a young man cannot stop. Love is one of those things."

By this time, Roland and I are so into his speech that we didn't care about the 100-degree weather that we were all sitting in.

He continued, "Love is something that man alone cannot control. Since you are both young men, you will be enticed by a woman to follow her wherever she goes. It is okay to do so, but just be smart about it. What I am trying to say is, I know I am going against what your Lola Alberta preaches, but it is okay to have a girlfriend at your age. Treat her with kindness, be strong for her, and be a gentleman. Take her out on small dates, hold her hand, pull her chair for her, and share your food."

Lolo continued by saying, "I am sure this is against everything your Lola Alberta has told you, but you know, it is okay to kiss a girl on the hand, on the forehead, the cheek, and also on the lips. You can kiss her there. But I will say this once: never kiss a girl down there!" He pointed to his pelvic area, and a slow, silent, but everlasting laugh emerged from this incredible, genuine, human being who I am so proud to say was my Lolo Felipe. Roland and I burst out in laughter as both of us continued to bond with our grandfather.

Halle Berries Smoothie
Yield: 2–3 servings

Ingredients

2 c. berries, fresh (strawberry, blueberry, blackberry)
1 c. red grapes, seedless
10 ice cubes
1 c. cranberry juice
1/2 banana
2 tbsp. honey

Procedure

1. Wash and clean all fruits/produce.
2. Place all ingredients in a blender; cover.
3. Blend until smooth.
4. If desiring a thicker smoothie, add entire banana to the blender.
5. Enjoy!

The Surfer
Yield: 2–3 servings

Ingredients

2 c. cantaloupe, cleaned, medium chunks
1 c. honeydew melon, cleaned, medium chunks
10 ice cubes
1 c. white grape juice
1/2 c. coconut milk
2 tbsp. honey

Procedure

1. Place all ingredients in a blender; cover.
2. Blend until smooth.
3. If a sweeter taste is desired, add more honey.
4. Enjoy!

Four

MAIN COURSE
MEMOIRS, EUROPEAN ADVENTURE

My father served in the US Army for over twenty years, and moving was part of our lives. We had moved six times during his term of service, so packing up, moving to a new location, going to a new school, and meeting new friends was not at all a problem. But this time, this move, was different. This was overseas. This was going to be a different country, different people, different food, different everything. We all read books that eased our minds, but we were still scared, scared of this big change. My dad was stationed in Heidelberg, West Germany (before the unification), from 1984–1988. These years are considered some of the best times of my life!

Eichbaum Stubchen Stories
Eichbaum Stubchen was a bar establishment in downtown Heidelberg that was a home away from home for many of us during the weekends. It was a place where—no matter who your friends were or who you hung out with, whether you were a jock, a smoker, a cheerleader, or just one of the guys—you were always welcome in this establishment.

A jolly old man would greet you at the door; that would be George, the owner/proprietor of the establishment. Whether he knew you or didn't care for you, you were always welcomed in. His sons would either and always be behind the bar serving the drinks or bringing drinks to the few tables in the pub, and his wife and workers would be in and out of the back room helping any way they could. This was Eichbaum.

The table and chairs were made of wood; nothing fancy at all about the craftsmanship, but it served its purpose. The bar was not too long, but again, it was always full. The smell of sweet perfume and cheap cologne always seemed to dance in the air with the smoke coming from cigarettes. This was Eichbaum.

You would always hear the latest gossip; good or bad, it didn't matter. You would forget about it anyways since you just drank your sixth shot of Captain Morgan or whatever poison it was that night. Every once in a while, you would make it to the back and head into the bathroom. But before the bathroom, you would look at the jukebox and never put money in it because you were saving that last "funf mark" for your last liter of beer for the night. You always thought someone else would put money in the jukebox. This was Eichbaum.

Sometimes you would tell George that you will be coming back and step outside on the Hauptstrasse. You would meet friends that had a little something that would enhance the evening's activity, whether it was a bottle of strawberry champagne, a shot of Captain Morgan, bottled beer or whatnot, we all would enter back with that extra laughter we did not have earlier. This was Eichbaum.

Even when the night was still young, but if you had way too much to drink and George would notice that your eyes could be blindfolded by dental floss, he would take the final pint glass away from you and give you black coffee instead. "Dreeenk vis," he'd command in his German accent. You wouldn't argue and just obey. This was Eichbaum. Since many wonderful memories have been brought to my attention by many Heidelberg High School alumni, I have decided to include many of their fond, memorable moments from this unforgettable establishment called Eichbaum Stubchen.

TODD MCCLEARY, CLASS OF '87

I can remember so many things but not too much details. One thing I do remember vividly is the jukebox in the back by the bathrooms. The one song I remember is "Tainted Love" by Soft Cell and how the whole bar would sing along with that song. That was awesome! The other thing I can remember is boot races. The last thing I will add is there was this guy (can't remember his name, but can picture his face) who would pierce his face if you bought him a beer.

MICHAEL RILEY, CLASS OF '89

I am not sure if I am the only kid who did this, but I went down there regularly; and my parents had absolutely no idea what I was doing. If they knew I was going to a bar, they probably would have flipped out! I am sure you will get plenty of comments about George and everyone's affection for him. The best part about going to Eichbaum was that on any given Friday or Saturday night, you knew that you could walk in and hang out with friends. It would not have mattered where it was or what type of business it was, but the fact that there was a place known to all that we could hang out, have fun, and connect with one another as American kids living thousands of miles from our "home" was what mattered.

So much time has passed that I am sure I have forgotten more of the fun times than I remember. Anyway, here is a ramble of my memories. One of my most fond memories was the Captain Morgan challenge. There was a running list of who could drink the most Captain Morgan shots. Tony G. and I were both pretty high on the list, and I remember a couple of nights when we kept trying to surpass each other. I could not handle a lot of alcohol at that age, but for some reason, Captain Morgan went down easy; and it took quite a few to get me hammered. I can't even touch the stuff now. I also remember a couple of HHS classmates having sex on the floor of the men's room. I will omit the names to protect the guilty. They were of course both drunk, and for a sixteen-year-old who didn't have much experience in that area, it certainly was an awakening. The atmosphere of alcohol, no parents, and all that freedom in a relatively safe environment really helped me to grow up faster and become more mature than I would have in a stateside setting.

ROMMEL MENDOZA, CLASS OF '88
I remember the first time I ever stepped foot in this ever so popular hangout. I had met the owner, George, when I was fifteen. I went downtown on a Friday, late August evening, with a small group of friends. I was introduced to George, the proprietor of the establishment, at the entrance of Eichbaum. He was a short, older, German, chubby fellow and charming as can be. He was very nice to those who entered his bar but, with the help of his son behind the bar, "laid the law down" for those unruly bastards who could not hold their alcohol down and became belligerent in his fine establishment. Anyways, we spoke quite a bit about where I was from, high school, and sports. I was still in front of the entrance, outside, while he was inside the door guarding it like a watchdog. I was very eager to get in since everyone that I knew was inside already having their first beer.

As soon as I motioned to go in, he asked me with his deep German accent, "Rommel, how old are you?"

I didn't want to lie to this gentleman, so I honestly answered, "I am fifteen, and my birthday is next week."

He looked at me and smiled. "I cannot let you in since you are only fifteen."

I looked at him, and without even arguing, I said, "Okay, I understand."

But I didn't leave. For the next couple of hours, I remained outside, in front of Eichbaum, and spoke with George. He even offered me soda while we chatted outside.

As I was about to leave, he shook my hand and said, "You come back next week, and I will have your beer waiting for you."

I smiled and said, "Thank you, I will see you next week!" The rest is history.

CATHY VAN VOORHIS, CLASS OF '89
As I am about to turn forty, I have caught myself looking back on my formidable years and extraordinary life lessons and mentors I have had that have shaped my life as I know it far. Even though it's just an old German building in downtown Heidelberg—most likely a serious health code violation in today's standards—a bar full of stale beer smell and old smoke, I still consider this place a major influence in my life. Not a person or specific memory but the essence of a place I grew up with that taught me more about life, how to be in the world, as well as consequences of choices we make—and don't make—was at Eichbaum.

Unlike in the USA, growing up in Europe as a military brat is an experience like no other. Kids are taught respect for other cultures, respect for elders (a very tight community of extended family), but most of all respect for no-drinking age. Living within American rules but having the benefits of being surrounded by another culture opened up many opportunities most kids don't get the experience of having. Extensive travel to other countries being the most fun I remember. As I got to be high-school age—okay, maybe junior-high age, as more responsibility and trust is a natural part of growing up, the subject of drinking comes up and of no-drinking age and how to handle it or not.

In Germany, there isn't a drinking age and I took full advantage of that freedom! My first visit to Eichbaum, I was in my junior varsity cheerleading uniform with my best friends at a very tender age. With ten marks, we asked George, the bar-keep, what was good and he taught us the essence of beer in all of its categories with taste tests by starting us off light with a pilsner. We definitely spent way more than ten marks, but we stayed for hours as some kind of courtesy and welcome to the Eichbaum family. Giggling and goofy, we most likely discussed the ways of the world (about our parents and teachers hassling us and about boys we liked and how we'd pass them origami-folded notes) and "solved problems" within the time it took to get buzzed and home on the bus before the streetlights went out before curfew.

Life lessons from Eichbaum include:

1. It was a private club, but everyone was welcome; no prejudices or differences existed inside those doors.
2. Always buy your friends a beer; they will always buy you one too.
3. Make friends with every table; it makes for much more fun.
4. Meet people from different backgrounds. You will be happy you did.
5. If your friend starts a drunken fight, stand up for them.
6. If you start a drunk fight, you'll need someone to stand up for you.
7. Beer goggles are universal, hangovers are too.
8. The Turks sitting at the church aren't handing out candy.
9. If you eat their candy, have a friend's house to crash.
10. George was like a cool uncle watching out for us.
11. Cobblestones make you trip and fall after one visit.
12. The bus and taxis were the only mode of transportation.
13. Serious creativity and enlightenment was born from that bar.
14. Tequila shots aren't like lemonade, but after one, it's not that bad.
15. If you're overserved, sitting sideways in the backseat with the heat full blast will make you spin dizzy; then puke into your umbrella.
16. Blaming that tequila-smelling puke on the door on food poisoning doesn't work for most parents. Cleaning up the car the next day will resolve that from ever happening again though. Long story short, just stick to Eichbaum beer!

I can go into many details of these life experiences, both sad and silly, that define my foggy memory; but overall, the friendships, bonding, love, sometimes hate, jealously, plots of revenge, secrets, crushes, old heartbreaks, new heartthrobs, paying it forward when you had money, learning how to ask for a loan when you didn't have the currency of life and living was developed in this dusty, dirty old bar. Eichbaum was a place where everyone belonged, and nobody was a stranger. I try to recreate Eichbaum in all places I go in the world today.

As an adult, I always sit down next to someone sitting alone at a bar and offer to buy them a beer and offer conversation in case they need a friend. The subject of growing up in Germany usually comes up and opens up a world of conversation. Even without knowing it, Eichbaum taught me how to live generously in the world and blessed me by staying in touch like we all have throughout the years, and that is priceless!

Thank you for giving me the chance to share how Eichbaum enriched my life! Prost!

Rob "Roo" Robbins, Class of '88
Growing up, my high school friends meant everything to me. We spent almost every free hour together playing basketball, football, going downtown for drinks, and any other reason to get together and talk what we could think of. Our group had a name and a place—the Boyz, and Eichbaum's what defined us. Eich's was our place to drink, talk, and come together as a group. George, the owner, knew us by name and remembered us years later when we would come back during college breaks. For us, Eich's was our place to start a good night in Heidelberg. Even now, I can remember the wooden bar, the tight layout, and the many nights of partying with the greatest friends I've ever had. Fittingly, in a country and place where not much changes, Eich's is no more. I visited Heidelberg many years ago, and at first, I was disappointed it was no longer there. Then I realized that it will always live on in our collective thoughts and stand for something great that we all had together. We'll never forget! Prost to all the Boyz!

Kenneth Johnson, Class of '88
Rommel and I were talking with George, the owner, just outside of Eichbaum. Now I do not know what had happened, but some dude started causing problems inside the establishment. George politely excused himself. He called out to his son behind the bar, who in turn swiftly removed the ruffian from inside Eichbaum. While grabbing behind the ruffian's neck and holding on to his left arm, his son escorted him across the Hauptstrasse to this enormous church made out of stone. He slammed the guy into the church, let him go, and casually walked back inside Eichbaum and politely asked who needed a beer. Who needs the police when you had your son there!

Katy Tomlinson Kavanagh, Class of '98
I was fortunate enough to spend all four years of high school at Heidelberg American High School in Heidelberg, Germany. I was equally as fortunate to have parents who understood that my brother,

Michael, and I were bound to drink, living in Germany. I can truly say that Eichbaum was our "Cheers." Everyone, including the bartender, Peter, knew our names. Peter was special to us because he could remember the drinks people liked. For instance, he knew that I always had an amaretto when I got to the bar and that I would switch to Hefeweizen after. My brother always drank Jack Daniel's and Coke. Peter could be a very stern guy as well if we got out of line. He wouldn't put up with any fighting or rowdy behavior. To put this all into perspective, you need to remember that we were seventeen and fifteen years old, respectively, and that our parents picked us up from this place every weekend night. They were nice enough to wait at a parking garage nearby, as to not embarrass us, but we were teenagers living at home, going to school on an army base.

I graduated from HHS in 1998, and I can remember that after the baccalaureate church service at the Heiliggeistkirche across the street, we convinced my parents to go with us into Eichbaum for the first time ever—to have a shot of tequila! Peter was serving cake there. He met my parents and had a conversation in broken Germ-lisch (German/English) about what good kids my brother and I were, which we thought was pretty funny. I remember, even then, thinking what a special experience we had during high school. We moved back to the Midwest soon after this; I went off to college in Wisconsin, and my brother went to a much more boring and sober high school experience in Minnesota.

I returned to Heidelberg twice in that first year: once at Christmas and then for graduation in May. I remember Eichbaum being open still at Christmas of 1998, but by the time I made it back for graduation, they had closed. I went there looking for Peter and miraculously found him, but not in the bar. He was working in one of the shops under the Heiliggeistkirche across the street, selling knickknacks. He remembered me, and even remembered that I drank amaretto. Tears came to his eyes when I approached him, and he hugged me. Anyone who knew Peter would know this was strange, because he was quite a stern guy normally; he often acted like he didn't like the Amis (Americans) who came to his bar. I believe that anyone who went to Heidelberg High after Eichbaum's closed in 1999 missed out on a true institution.

Oktoberfest

Oktoberfest is another special memory amongst my many travels. Taking place at the end of September and the beginning of October, this festival is one of the largest fairs in the world and is a time to celebrate the beers made in Munich, although this celebration is shared by people from all over the world. Only certain breweries are allowed to display their beer, and they must each meet certain requirements to be served during Oktoberfest.

Wandering through the grounds was just another of my world experiences that I will always remember. The sound of many different languages rang out like I was attending a meeting of the United Nations. People from every continent and many different countries had representatives there; the festival environment made us all one people for the time we shared there. With over thirty tents, there were all kinds of smells and sounds coming at me from all different directions. First I could hear traditional

German folk music, which reminded me much of polka music. Then, as I kept walking, I would hear a German rock band blaring from another tent.

Mixing in with these sounds were the various smells from the different types of foods served at each tent. I would be walking and would smell, and of course stop and taste, the strudels and pastries. Then, the smell of different kinds of cheeses would pass my nose. Then, the odor of barbequing pork knuckles would float by. With the addition of roasting duck, chicken, and sausage, I was overwhelmed with so many smells—all of them tempting. I didn't know how to fill my stomach since the festival was supposed to be about the beer, but the smells made me reconsider my priorities. Although food and beer is enough for a festival, the upbeat mood of the environment was what really made this an unforgettable experience. With people from all over the world dancing, singing, and enjoying each other, it was easy to forget all the differences we had between us. I had to be sure to show restraint though. The beer at Oktoberfest has more alcohol than average German beer and also has a much higher sugar content, as well. For this reason, it is easy to overindulge if you are not careful. Luckily, I was conscious of this difference and although I drank my fair share of beer, I was lucky to keep from numbering myself among the "Bierleichen." The literal translation to this is "beer corpses" and it refers to the drunken, passed-out people littered among the grounds. Luckily, there was a strong medical presence there to watch out for this very problem.

All in all, this experience will rank high in my memories and taught me that all kinds of people can come together, and food and drink is a great way to make this happen. Perhaps this is why I have chosen the career that I have today because I know that food and drink can create a bridge over any differences that people might have.

"The Boyz"

We were a savvy group of young individuals; each unique in his own way. We all had our own way of talking. Some were more quiet than others, some more boisterous. Some ate more than others, and some just ate cheese sandwiches. A few had bigger heads than others (the Big Head people, I will never forget that) and a couple had farts that would clear the entire back of the bus. One could sleep anywhere, everywhere, no matter how loud it may be. Some were smaller, others were taller. A few were slower, others were fast, and one could run like the wind. A few had their driver's license while a couple of us didn't mind sitting shotgun or calling out, "Back seat, behind the driver!" Some of us lived on post (Patrick Henry Village or Mark Twain Village) while others lived on the economy (living outside Patrick Henry Village or Mark Twain Village). We were a unique group of people with different races, religions, colors, and beliefs.

We did have many similarities as well. We were all athletes. For most of us, we all met at the Patrick Henry Village middle school basketball courts. Familiar faces soon became familiar names. We were basketball, baseball, football players, and ran track. We played manhunt, camped out in the Patrick Henry Village fields, and worked at Burger King. We drank lemon-lime California coolers and Bartles

& Jaymes when they came out with different flavors. German beer, shots, and the infamous Captain Morgan soon became our poison at the local drinking establishment called Eichbaum. We had classes together, sat at the same lunch table, and the flat between second and third floor was our little nesting ground before classes started. We skipped classes together, went to the casino to have breakfast, or just slept in someone's car during first period. WE STARTED THE BOW ZONE! Then everyone started doing it, even the females of the school. We made our mark!

One by one, year after year, we started to graduate. Class of '87, '88, '89, and '90 are all representatives in our unique group. As they say, all good things come to an end. But does it really? As I mentioned earlier, we are a savvy group of individuals, not so young anymore. I am happy to say since 1984 to 1985, our friendship, our brotherhood has been kept alive! Even before MySpace, Facebook, Twitter, Instagram became part of all our lives, we have been in touch. Some people ask how we have been in touch for such a long time. We all don't really know how to answer them. I think it's an overseas thing, a DODD's thing, it's a Heidelberg American High School thing. Thank you, my brothers, for being the boys we were and the men we are today.

France: Representing the USA

I was fourteen years old at the time. We had already been living in Heidelberg, West Germany, for over a year and already started turning acquaintances into friendships with several of the neighborhood kids. I did say West Germany; during this time, up until 1989, the country of Germany was still divided: East and West Germany. East Germany was still considered a Communist Bloc country, controlled by the USSR, etc…well, you get my point. Anyways, I played sports back in the United States and continued to do so after we settled in to our new housing unit in Patrick Henry Village. Baseball and basketball were my forte. I never played organized football but loved backyard football. It was the start of spring training for baseball, and I heard about tryouts for a traveling team. Tryouts for the baseball season did not start until mid-March. I thought this would be a good time to get a good jump on training for the season. A good friend of mine, Alex, asked if I wanted to try out with him. I, of course, did not hesitate. If you know Germany, during late February to early March, the weather is not the best. The weather was wet and cold. There were all sorts of guys trying out for the team, some freshman and a couple of sophomores. I knew a few of the guys but eventually would get to know all of them during the three-day tryouts. Your fingers would be numb from the cold air, and you had to keep moving to keep warm while fielding fly-balls or grounders. I remembered trying out in the infield. I played third and second base in the States, so I tried out for those positions. Coach Jones did not let up once. He was belting the balls, one after the other, harder and harder. Two, maybe three, got past me, but I think I did okay. Several of us then got moved to the outfield; I was one of them. There were others on the team who did a tad bit better than I did in the infield. Oh well, the outfield wasn't so bad. It was my turn to try out for center field. I caught the balls easily and ran like the wind when it came to running down fly balls. But what impressed Coach Jones and Coach Gonzales the most was my arm. I had a cannon for an arm!

Prix Fixe: Made in the USA by a Filipino

After each day of tryout, I would walk home since the field was only half of a mile away from my house. While living in the Patrick Henry Village, PHV is what everybody called it, there was a truck that sold German goodies. I later found out that this was the *brotchen* truck and inside was the *brotchen* lady that ran the operation. I finally gave in and approached this weird yet fascinating truck operation. As soon as you were close enough, the smell of sweet candy, bread, and other items floated in the air. I had to buy something. There were so many choices. I ended up buying gummies (Now I hope you all pronounced it correctly!). This was the start of a relationship with this dear old *brotchen* lady. After each day of tryouts, I looked for the *brotchen* lady. She would always be at the same spot every day. Cherry gummies, cola gummies, worms, smurf gummies—you name it, she had it! I would eventually stop buying the gummies from her. As you got older in Germany, you would learn of places to get things, and one of those places was the Gummie Basement. Anyways, other than gummies, *brotchen*, which is the national bread of Germany, became one of my usual buys. *Brotchen* are German bread rolls with a firm and crispy crumb but a soft and elastic inside. They are best to eat warm with your favorite jam, cheese, or better yet make it into sandwich; I did that often. Oh, how I miss having authentic German *brotchen*! Anyways, back to the story. After the third day of tryouts, I got the call back. I made the team! We were headed to St. Foy, France, and representing the United States in an international baseball tournament.

The bus ride to St. Foy was long and exhausting but exciting. How many teenagers do you know get to experience something like this! Rather than staying in hotels during the weeklong international baseball tournament, we paired up; and each pair was going to stay with host French families. Out of all the families who hosted international players, we soon realized that Alex (one of my teammates) and I had the best family: a dad, mom, and three children. I do want to add that the children consisted of one boy, maybe twelve years old, and two daughters, who were sixteen and seventeen years of age. The older of the two daughters was able to speak English clearly, but we had a bit of a communication barrier when speaking with the rest of the family. Let's see, two American fourteen-year-olds staying in a very nice house with two teenage, older daughters. You get the picture. Anyways, we were treated like royalty in their house. Other than having a beautiful home, the family also owned a small vineyard. Every single night, we were fed like long lost family members. From *boeuf bourguignon*, chicken fricassee, *coq au vin* to *gratin dauphinois*, ratatouille, roasted chicken provencal was served. These were only a few items I could remember. We ate like princes and drank wine from their vineyard like kings. Even though we may not have been able to communicate well, when it came to dinnertime, the communication barrier seemed to be nonexistent. We ate well!

Other than playing in the tournament during the day and eating like royalty when dinner was served, Alex and I were introduced to something new, something that we both have never experienced in our early stages of being a teenager. From the very first evening to the last night, an hour or so after dinner, a question would be asked from one of the daughters, "You like discotec?" The first time we heard that question, Alex and I looked at each other and asked, "What is a discotec?" They both smiled, and the older daughter said, "It's a place where we go and dance." "Sure, why not, let's go!" Other than being introduced to the club scene for the very first time, we were introduced to the "pregame" scene.

They took us to a quaint bar called Victor Hugos, and that is where I was introduced to my first gin and tonic. It was the night of many "firsts" this evening. First night of staying with the most awesome of French families, the first time eating very delicious French cuisine, first time drinking gin and tonic (to this day, I still drink it), first time going into a bar and ordering a drink, first time going to a club (after a few gin and tonics, I didn't care how I looked dancing), and first time kissing a French girl; Sylvia was her name, and it was the sixteen-year-old daughter. I am assuming that is where the term *French-kissing* came from! As the week progressed, we were winning our games, continued to eat like kings, and partied like rock stars. The question of going out to the "discotec" became obsolete; we just got ready to go at a certain time.

At the close of the week, we lost the championship game to Spain 2–1. It went into extra innings, but Spain prevailed. Our team did manage to receive two awards. Ricky Gittens (rest in peace, my friend) was awarded the MVP award. This guy basically hit a home run every single time he stepped up to the plate. Teams soon realized to walk him rather than having a baseball soar over their heads and into the farmer's field. Joey Gonzales also received an award for most outstanding pitcher. This player had a cannon for an arm and a curveball that made players duck every time he threw it. I was fourteen at the time of this tournament, but I can still see the baseball field in the middle of the farmer's field and the makeshift dugout that was built to accommodate the players during their game. The big red tent in the distance that housed international players was where we all sat and waited for our turn on the field. The smell of burgers, bratwurst, and French baguettes lingered in the air throughout the tournament. I can close my eyes and can still see it all.

Whatever happened to Sylvia you may ask. After the tournament ended, we said our good-byes and kept in touch for a while via mail. Back then, *e-mail* was not even found in the dictionary. I then slowly stopped responding to her mail. I started to date someone else. I did manage to see her again when we were invited once again to participate in the international tournament the following year. She saw me at Victor Hugos as we arrived into town. She greeted me as how the French do, and that was it. The coaches and teammates looked at me; I just smiled. Later I found out that she hated me since I stopped writing to her. I also figured this out since every time I stepped up to the plate, I could hear her say, "Hit him," or was it, "I hate him!" Her English was better by this time.

Bistek Tagalog (Beefsteak)
Yield: Serves 6–8

Ingredients

2 lb. beef sirloin, thinly sliced
1/2 c. soy sauce
3 tbsp. lemon or lime juice
2 tsp. sesame oil
1 tbsp. garlic, fresh, minced
1/2 tsp. garlic powder
1/2 tsp. ground black pepper
1 large onion, sliced into rings
4 tbsp. canola oil
1 c. bell peppers, sliced (optional)
1 c. string beans (optional)
salt and black pepper (to taste, if needed)

Procedure

1. Marinate sliced beef in soy sauce, lemon (or lime) juice, sesame oil, garlic, garlic powder, and ground black pepper for at least 2–4 hours. Overnight is best.
2. Heat saute pan on medium high; add oil. Carefully place marinated beef in heated pan (without marinade). Saute beef until browned on both sides, about 3–5 minutes. Set aside, keep warm.
3. Using the same pan, saute sliced onions and any added vegetables (bell peppers and/or string beans) for 2 minutes. Add the marinade and bring to a boil.
4. Turn heat down to medium and add cooked beef.
5. Allow to simmer for 15–20 minutes or until meat is tender. Add water, if needed.
6. Add salt and black pepper, if needed.
7. Serve hot and over jasmine rice. Enjoy.

Chicken Tinola

Yield: 4–6 bowls

Ingredients

2 lb. chicken pieces (drums, wings, and/or thighs)

2 tbsp. vegetable or canola oil

2 tbsp. garlic, fresh, chopped

1/4 c. onions, medium dice

3 tbsp. ginger, peeled, thinly sliced on a bias

8 c. water

2 c. chayote, peeled, deseeded (may substitute with russet potatoes, peeled, cleaned, quartered)

1 c. green beans, cleaned

2 c. spinach, fresh

3–4 tbsp. fish sauce

Procedure

1. Rinse chicken pieces of any impurities. Set aside.
2. Using a stockpot large enough to hold chicken, place on stove, turn heat to medium high, and add oil.
3. When oil is heated, add garlic and onions. Saute for five minutes; add chicken.
4. Cook chicken until lightly browned; add ginger. Saute for another five minutes.
5. Add 4 cups of water; stir chicken and scrape bottom of pot, if needed, to add the extra flavor from sautéed chicken. Add 1 tablespoon of fish sauce and remaining 4 cups of water.
6. Continue to cook chicken on medium-high heat until water begins to boil. Turn heat down to medium; add 1 tablespoon of fish sauce. Stir and continue to cook for five minutes.
7. Add chayote, green beans, and remaining fish sauce and gently stir; cover pot with lid. Allow to cook for 10–15 minutes or until beans and chayote are tender.
8. Add spinach and turn heat down to low. Place lid on pot. Let simmer for five minutes.
9. Taste soup; add more fish sauce if needed. Turn stove off.
10. Serve in soup bowls with cooked rice noodles (Filipino pho) or jasmine rice on the side.
11. Enjoy!

Prix Fixe: Made in the USA by a Filipino

41

Pork Adobo over Linguini

Yield: 3–5 servings

Mushroom Tomato Ragu

2 tbsp. olive oil
1 c. Roma tomato, small dice
1/2 c. yellow onion, small dice
1 tbsp. garlic, fresh, minced
3/4 c. green onion
1 c. sliced mushrooms
1 tbsp. basil, fresh, chopped
1 tsp. dry oregano
1 tsp. black pepper
1 tsp. kosher salt
1/4 c. pasta water

1/2 box linguini
6 c. water
1 tbsp. kosher salt
1/2 c. pasta water
1 tbsp. olive oil
1 tsp. butter
1/2 tsp. Italian seasoning

5–10 pieces prepared pork adobo with sauce, cooked, warm
1/4 c. pork adobo sauce, cooked, warm
1 tbsp. green onion, chopped (garnish)
1 tbsp. Roma tomato, small dice (garnish)

Procedure

1. Place water in a medium pot. Once water starts to boil, add salt and pasta. Follow instructions on box for correct doneness; usually 8–10 minutes for al dente. Strain cooked pasta, making sure to save pasta water. Keep warm; set aside.
2. Heat olive oil in a saute pan to medium-high heat; add onion and garlic. Saute for two minutes, add mushrooms. Continue to saute for another five minutes.

3. Add tomatoes, fresh basil, oregano, black pepper, and salt; saute for five minutes. When ragu starts to dry, add pasta water, mix, and turn heat down to low.

4. Heat a medium saute pan; melt butter and add olive oil. Carefully place 1/2 cooked pasta in saute pan, add 1/2 Italian seasoning over pasta. Using tongs, toss to combine pasta with seasoning, butter, and olive oil.

5. Add 2 tablespoons of pork adobo sauce to the pasta. Again, using tongs, toss to combine sauce with pasta.

6. Add half of the ragu mixture to pasta and five chunks of warm, cooked adobo over pasta; carefully toss pork adobo, ragu, and pasta together, making sure to break pork adobo to small pieces. Using tongs, place on serving plate(s).

7. Garnish with green onions and fresh diced tomatoes.

8. Depending on serving size, the recipe will allow for another serving or two.

9. Taste, share, and enjoy!

Five

MAIN COURSE
MEMOIRS, LATIN STYLE

España

Living in Europe during your high school years had its ups and downs, but I can honestly say the negativity of living in Germany started to diminish as I went up the ranks in high school, turning from a lower classman to an upper classman. Even though you could sneak a beer or a shot when you were fourteen or so, turning sixteen meant a little freedom in the public's eye. At this age, you could sit in a pub, a tavern, or a bar and have a drink, a shot, or a mixture of both and not worry about someone looking at you in a weird, underage way. At this age, you could enter Eichbaum's and sit with your friends and have that liter of beer that you saw and heard stories about. At this age, you were considered an upper classman. At this age, you could go to the pinnacle of spring break destinations—Lloret de Mar, Spain!

Going to Spain for spring break was on every student's mind. Lloret de Mar was considered the Daytona Beach/Miami for those stateside college students, but much better. Why? Well, over 90 percent of the inhabitants in Llloret de Mar, for one week in March or April, were high school students from American high schools in Europe doing what high school students do best *without* parents. I will leave that answer to the imagination!

There were two choices on how to get to Spain: the school-sponsored bus trip or through the travel agency, also by bus. My posse and I decided on the travel agency; not sure why, but hey, we were en route to our paradise. We boarded the bus at the Patrick Henry Village middle school parking lot. Most of the passengers on the bus were high school students, but there were several couples on there, recent Heidelberg graduates who waited just as long for this trip, and a few older passengers who had no idea the ride they were about to encounter was something they were not ever going to forget. As soon as the bus pulled out of the parking lot, the first bottle of German Pilsner was popped open. My group sat in the back of the bus along with several HHS alumni. We all raised our beers up and shouted, "Prost!" It was going to be a long ride but an adventure we would never forget!

The trip from Heidelberg to Lloret de Mar, with the rest stops and fuel fill-up, took a good fourteen hours or so. Our first stop was in Lyon, France. I have been to France before which, is in another chapter in this book. We took advantage of the thirty-minute stop by loading up on your usual high school food: chips, beef jerky, gum, and, of course, liquor. I remember buying a bottle of apple corn while one of my partners in crime purchased some banana liquor. We boarded the bus, and we continued our journey. Not knowing at the time the highway or route the bus was taking at the time, we did pass some very notable cities in France: Lyon, Avignon, Montpellier, Perpignan, and parts of the Pyrennes mountain range that would eventually take us to our destination.

By the fourth hour, mostly everyone in the back of the bus were already passed out from drinking. I remember having headphones on and loudly singing along to the New Edition's *Under the Blue Moon* cassette tape in my Walkman. Every once in a while, someone would yell out, "Shut the f—— up!" I didn't hear anything. I continued with my singing until I fell asleep.

We finally arrived in Lloret de Mar early in the morning. We checked in to our hotel room and headed to—a bar, no, the beach, no. We decide to head to the cliffs and climb them. Yeah, quite stupid and dangerous, but we were in Spain. It took us a good hour or so to get from one side of the cliffs to the other. We built up quite an appetite, so we stopped at a fast-food establishment and ordered what an average high school student would eat: burger, fries, and soda. The burger was good but definitely tasted different. I later found out that they used *bull* meat and not the average cattle they use here in the USA. It was actually leaner, not too much fat. The fries were a good accompaniment but the use of mayo and ketchup together brought them to life! We then stopped at a *helado* (ice cream) shop and was able to sample just about all the flavors they had to offer. The cute girl who was working behind the counter was very friendly to us, even though we ended up not buying anything. The ice cream was so fresh in flavor. Chunks of fresh strawberry were easily seen from one sample. With my broken Spanish and my vague understanding of the language, I was able to learn that the ice cream was *casero* or "homemade." It was very delicious.

We finished our meals and little dessert sampling and headed to Magic Kingdom, located in the center of Lloret de Mar. Magic Kingdom had a clublike atmosphere but was wide-open with video arcade games situated everywhere, a few bars located on each side, and the Jamaican Rasta men standing on the corner happily greeting you as you walked by them. They were there for one reason. Smile!

During spring break at Lloret de Mar, my group and I were introduced to Spanish Sangria, the Scorpion, and Dr. Funk. These were all beverages that would warm you up and keep you warm all night long. The Evolution, Fame, Texas Saloon, the Polynesian were all bars and clubs that kept the evening going and turned night slowly into day. Just like spring break stateside, you would meet others from different schools. Even though you may have been rivals during the school year, being in Spain during spring break, everyone put their differences aside for that one week of fun and debauchery.

Other than the burgers (I think that is what we ate every single day—all week), the new drinks we learned to make, the clubs, new people we met, one of the most important things I remember about Spain is the people who lived in this tiny section of Spain. The locals were very friendly. The cafes, restaurants, stores, etc., would open early in the morning. They would then close during the afternoon. This was known as their siesta. During this time, they would eat a little *merienda* (small snack), nap, and run errands. The shops, café, bars, etc., would then reopen at 4:00 p.m. and stay open until late evening. I didn't know at the time, but the little snacks that the cafés served are called tapas. Tapas can consist of all sorts of meats, seafood, vegetables but served in bite-size pieces. You would usually order at least four to five different tapas and share it among family or friends who were sitting with you.

Even though I have only been to Spain once, the fun I had with my friends in Lloret de Mar and the hospitality of the Spanish people will always be remembered. Lastly, my last name, *Mendoza*, comes from the Basque region of Spain. So the Spanish blood runs in my veins. That is why we are such hospitable, fun people to be around!

Tijuana, Mexico

I have been very fortunate to have visited the Baja California region of Mexico a few times. The Pacific Ocean seems a bit quieter in this area compared to its counterpart up north in San Diego and Los Angeles. Yes, I know it's the same ocean but not as many people, cars, or even tourists. It looked more pure, at times untouched. Anyways, back to reality. I first visited the Baja region of Mexico many, many years ago in this city, a city called Tijuana. You may have heard of it. Back then, it was safe to park your car in the USA side, walk about one mile, then go through the rotating gates. You then entered a different world. You could tell you were not in San Diego County anymore. More trash and debris were seen on every corner. Young children would be running up to you selling gum to make some money, cabdrivers hawking potential passengers but patiently waiting. The smell of history along with aromas of fried food, sautéed vegetables, carne asada, and handmade tortillas filled the air. This city was alive; this was Tijuana, Mexico.

The city of Tijuana was far from looking like San Diego but very eclectic and alive in its own way. It is busy like New York City: locals walking everywhere, the sounds of car horns every five seconds, and food vendors on every street corner. I remember tasting my first taco from Tijuana from a street vendor who was situated outside this rather famous club. It's a place that played great music, had beautiful women, and had nonstop action. I will leave the name out, but for those of you who have been to this city, you know the place or places, ha ha ha! After enjoying a night away with my cousin, brother, and friends, a sweet aroma of cooked meat floated in the air that seemed to hypnotize all of us. We were all hungry and quickly walked to the street vendor. The smoke grew as we got closer to the food vendor; the beautiful aroma of carne asada quickly became one with our noses. We were all hungry; and while in Rome—or should I say in Tijuana, we did as the locals did: we ate street tacos. I ordered two carne asada tacos and one taco carnita. These were handmade corn tortilla tacos, made at a pushcart, by a food vendor, in Tijuana, Mexico. It did not get more authentic than this. They were delicious!

Another time in Tijuana was my first experience drinking the local tequila. Now we all know that the normal way of taking a shot is with a shot glass. Not in this local club. We sat close to the stage. This should give you an idea of the type of place this establishment may be. Music is blaring, the lights are dim, the smell of alcohol mixed with sweet fruit was in the air. We ordered a round of beers and started enjoying the sights and sounds of the club. Before taking another gulp of my beer, an hombre, who was marching around the club with a whistle in his mouth, blowing it like a madman with a bottle in each of his hands, came up to our table. He happened to stand behind me first, and everyone was looking at me. I had no clue what was going on. Before I had a chance to turn around, he tilted my head back, while blowing his whistle of course, and proceeded to pour a shot of the local tequila in my mouth. When in Rome, I mean, Tijuana, do what the locals do. He filled my mouth halfway with tequila, tilts my head forward, and then shakes it! He then asked me, "Te gusto naranja?" which translates to "Do you like orange?" The other bottle in his other hand was orange juice. I nodded my head yes, and he proceeds again with his ritual: tilted my head back, filled my mouth with tequila and orange juice, tilted my head forward, then shook, tilted my head back, filled my mouth with tequila… This went on for at least four episodes. The hombre quickly walked away from our table, still blowing his whistle, and looked for his next victim elsewhere in the club. One of my friends had paid for the "tequila show," and they all had smirks on their faces. This was my first time doing this, and they all said, "Welcome to Tijuana!"

The third time I visited Tijuana was during the daytime. I went there with two friends and wanted to buy some souvenirs for family and friends back home. One of my friends who lived in San Diego took us to the shopping district of Tijuana. It was more of a long, narrow street that had small family-owned shops on both sides of the street. From one store to another, each owner sold things form conch shells to ponchos, from paper mache to T-shirts, CDs, and US-branded clothing. You bartered with the owners until a price was agreed upon. It reminded me a lot of the Philippines and its markets. After shopping, I had to get one last taste of the local eats. I had to try what the Baja region was known for: its seafood. We were able to stumble across a café. I ended up ordering fish tacos with a bottle of Corona to wash it down. The fish tacos were lightly battered and wrapped in a corn tortilla. Shredded lettuce, fine cheddar cheese, and fresh salsa finished the entrée. The fish was delicate. Since the fish was lightly breaded, you could taste the freshness of the product. The fresh salsa added a nice piquant flavor to the taco. I was now content with all my visits to this big city. This was my cherry on top.

Ensenada, Mexico

After a night of mayhem in Tijuana, we all woke up in our car—thankfully on the USA side of the border. I had no clue how we all got back to the car, but from what one of my friends said, it was all worth it! They were all deciding that we needed to shower first. I was still a mess. That damn hombre with the tequila bottle ruined me. My head was pounding, and I needed food, something greasy to be exact, to get this feeling of vomit out of me. We were not checked in a hotel since we decided to go straight to Tijuana after our drive from Las Vegas. So now you had four guys who smelled like last night's dinner, liquor, and clubbing—all looking for someplace to shower. Someone mentioned the local YMCA in San Diego. So we asked for directions and drove around. This is before GPS, so we relied on our memory, which at this time was totally shot. We gave up on that idea. Another friend suggested we jump the fence at a local hotel that had an outside pool. Still in pain, I smiled at that idea but didn't say anything on how stupid that sounded. After driving for fifteen minutes or so, we actually found a hotel with an outside pool. By this time, I was more coherent. One friend got out of the car with his towel in his hand; the three of us sat and watched to see if he would actually jump the fence. He placed his hand on the fence and slowly turned around and looked at us. "Come on, man, get out, let's go!" he yelled. We looked at him, and without hesitation, we all laughed! The three of us soon figured out that it was a dumb idea. They jokingly argued who thought of the idea. Since no one else had any other ideas, I came up with one.

"First, we eat. Second, since we all smell like shit, we are not here to impress anyone. After we eat, we head down to Ensenada, clean up, eat again, rest, and head out and party like rock stars." They all agreed. I was king for the hour after coming up with that blissful idea.

Our drive down to Ensenada was uneventful. Thinking that the toll on a one-lane highway was six dollars, we soon found out that it was six pesos, which at the time was less than a dollar. I do remember riding close to the shore. The Pacific Ocean has always been a favorite sight of mine. The drive to Ensenada from Tijuana took a little over one hour. We passed small pueblos, or towns, along the way, watching locals pulling their wagons to get from one point to another. These were areas away from the city, away from the hustle of the metropolitan. This was the old way of doing things. We knew we were getting close to the city of Ensenada because there were steadily more and more houses grouped together. The roads were wider, and more cars could be seen. We finally reached the Cinderella of the Pacific, a port city, Ensenada.

As mentioned earlier, we executed my plan after arriving in Ensenada. Rather than going to a local restaurant and eating the local grub, we decided we wanted something USA made or close to it. After walking a couple of blocks, we saw a good American sanctuary—Pizza Hut. Since it was a beautiful afternoon, we sat outside. A couple of the guys ordered soda; two of us ordered the local beer. To my surprise, it was not Corona. Tecate is their poison in these parts. It was the first time I had Tecate, and I can say that I still drink it to this day. Since pizza was on the menu, we decided to put other toppings on the pizza to jazz it up a bit. Since we were in Mexico, we wanted to spice it up a bit. The server told us that Ensenada had the best peppers in Mexico. I am not sure if he really did mean this since it was four gringos who were sitting there, but we obliged and said, "Add some peppers." After two cans of Tecate beer and going over what may have happened in Tijuana the night before, our pizza arrived: one with just pepperoni, the other was sausage with jalapeno and banana peppers. After the first bite of the pizza with the peppers, I was in love. It was the first time I had any peppers with pizza! The peppers did spice up the pizza quite a bit, but they were fresh; they did not come from a can. They seemed as if they were just picked that day. I didn't even bother taking a piece of the average, normal pizza that was also ordered.

Daylight soon turned to night. Our stomachs were full, and we were already buzzing from the beers we drank with our pizza. We changed into our club attire and headed out. As we stepped out of our hotel's front entrance, we realized that across the street was one of Ensenada's finest clubs—*wink, wink*. We scurried across the street like a group of Catholic school boys. The place was dim. Dance music was playing, and the smell of sweet perfume lingered in the air. It was not too busy, and the manager sat at a round table with plush seats. We were being treated like VIPs for some reason. Women of all shapes and sizes walked up, sat with us, and introduced themselves in broken English. A few didn't speak English, so every time someone spoke in Spanish, my friends would ask me what they said. The music was so loud in there, I would just smile, look at my friend, and say, "She said she likes you."

After a few cans of Tecate, a couple shots, and some flirting around, we decided to hit the town and see what the town had to offer. The once quiet street was now filled with cars cruising up and down the main strip. Just like any other beach town in the USA, they cruised the main strip in Ensenada. We saw a few people on the sidewalks walking, which we found a bit odd. It was almost midnight, and we were sure to see many more people out. People were already out in Tijuana by 9:00 p.m. We figured it was the same in Ensenada. We were so wrong! We heard music blasting from a corner club. We ran to it without haste. No one was in there. We heard more music just several feet away; no one was inside. Across the street, more music was heard. Again, no one was in each of the clubs we walked into. We walked two more blocks down the main strip, heard music blaring out from a club, and again no one was to be found. We stood at the corner and watched the cars cruise up and down the strip for the next thirty minutes with odd looks on our faces. We just couldn't understand. It was a Saturday night, and no one was in the clubs; everyone was just cruising up and down the strip. We finally decided to call it a night with confused looks on our faces.

My visit to these two cities was enjoyable. I have not been to this region for many years now but still can see the gates that separate Tijuana from its sister city of San Diego. I can still see the children tugging at my shirt asking me if I want to buy gum from them. I am sure the cabdrivers are still waiting for passengers. I can still see the old bull fighting arena that we drove by. I can still see the old Pintos, Oldmobiles, Fords, etc., cruising down the main strip. Every single time I see Tecate beer, it reminds me of Ensenada. By the way, I found out the next day that Ensenada is a couples destination, and many couples go there due to it being not as busy. It is also a port city. There were no cruise ships in port; Ensenada remained quiet all weekend long. The food, well, after having authentic Mexican and fresh peppers, it's difficult to find good Mexican fare anywhere else.

Puerto Rico One trip that I will never forget is the first time I visited Puerto Rico, in 2012. Known as La Isla del Encanto, or the Island of Enchantment, Puerto Rico is one of my favorite places to visit in the world. Because I was sent there by my employer, this trip involved as much work as it did play, but that is okay because I was sure to return for vacation later with my family. The two things that stood out most on this trip were the people and, of course, the food. Some of the friendliest people on this planet, the *Puertorriquenos*, had a way of always making me feel like family wherever I went. As a chef, though, I always like to get a feel for the local cuisine when I travel. The food in Puerto Rico had the same home-cooked feel to it as that of the food in the southern United States. I always felt the food was made with that special ingredient, TLC. Mofongo, one of their staple dishes, is made from mashed plantains and garlic, although each area had a different twist to this dish. In Raices, my cousin served me his version of mofongo, and it included sautéed jumbo shrimp and a side of mojo criollo, a garlicky onion and citrus blend. One dish that I had to try was one I saw on the Food Network show *Man v. Food* with Adam Richman. It is called chuleta de kan kan and is made up of pork chops, ribs, and fried pork skins; and it is served with a side of rice and black beans. This mouth-watering dish lived up to the hype on that show, and by the time I left the restaurant, only bare bones were left on my plate! Another place I was able to visit during my first trip to Puerto Rico was Bayamon. This area is known as El Pueblo del Chicharron, or Fried Pig Skin City. True to its nickname, this is where they roast whole pigs over a spit. The executive chef, who was one of the coolest chefs I ever worked with, was nice enough to show us the landmarks of the island; and this spot was one of the stops. Bayamon was about a thirty-minute drive from the city of San Juan. While driving up the mountainside, you would see open-air eateries on each side of the road. But there was one that was well-known for its roasted pig. We finally arrived and went straight to the window that had an entire roasted pig over hot coals roasting away. I was in roasted-pig heaven. For those of you who may not know, the Philippines is known to roast whole pigs, so I felt like I was home. But the true test was to taste and determine what was better. The chef went ahead and ordered for us all. From plantains, black beans, pickled vegetables, rice, and of course the roasted pig, we had a table with enough food for a village. The roasted pig was delicious. It reminded me of my uncles back home sitting around drinking beer while taking turns turning the roast. Which roasted pig is better: Puerto Rico or the Philippines? I plead the fifth.

On to happy hour from 3:00 p.m. to 7:00 p.m. at our hotel bar. Happy hour was not your normal happy hour. Rather than just well drinks, happy hour consisted of everything including top-shelf liquors like Patron, Black Label, Don Q Rum, and all the high-end liquor that you can think of. It didn't matter what day it was, my party and I were always the first to be seated at the bar at 3:00 p.m. We became regulars even though we were only there for less than a week.

While in San Juan, we were able to experience the city like most tourists our age did. We got to taste the local eats, drink the local drinks, and see the local sites. The food, the rum, and all the sites were fascinating. We learned that the pina colada was first invented in Puerto Rico. The best rums come from this island; and the local beer, Medalla, became our companion during the trip. It was after going out and exploring the city when I got the chance to really taste what Puerto Rican cuisine was all about. There was a diner about one hundred yards from our hotel that was open twenty-four hours a day that we frequented after our nightly outings. Tostones, *sopon de pollo con arroz* (chicken soup with rice), carne asada (beef stew), and much more were also on the menu. After a night of Don Q and Medalla in our system, any of the abovementioned food did the body good. For the week we were in Puerto Rico, we became regulars at the diner as well. At 2:00 a.m., the diner seemed to attract the same people: locals wanting something in their stomachs to ease the burden of alcohol the next day. My boys and I fitted right in. A smirk here and there would be heard from one of us as we talked about what had transpired during our evening out. During this time, my Spanish, which is not the best in the world, would come out. Jose, born and raised in El Salvador and my coworker at the time, would laugh and be amazed at the level of Spanish that was coming out of my mouth. He never knew I had it in me. But it was the alcohol talking, and it made the words flow out of my mouth so easy.

Second Trip to Puerto Rico

The second time I visited Puerto Rico was with my wife and son. I was on vacation. I told myself I would never take my wife to this enchanted place. I wanted to keep Puerto Rico to myself. It was going to be my place of escape, my serenity with some rum on the side. But after thinking about it, I wanted to be able to explore the island. And there is no better person to be with in exploring than my wife. She is such an adventurous person, and taking pictures is one of her hobbies. Since I didn't take any pictures on my first trip, I would leave all the picture taking to her.

Our first stop was Ponce, Puerto Rico. It was a good hour or so drive from San Juan airport but a nice drive. We drove through the middle of the island and enjoyed the drive through the mountains. Once in Ponce, we checked in to the resort and finally settled into our room. We opened the balcony door, and right in front of us was the blue waters of Mar Caribe, the Caribbean Sea. I felt a bit ashamed for being in such a great resort. Here we were in 75-degree tropical weather with the cool breeze from the sea hitting our faces; while back home, our family was sitting at home in single-digit weather. Since it was the first week after Christmas break, there were hardly any tourists on the resort. You could count the number of tourists at one time with the number of fingers and toes you had. The resort was ours for the next few days.

Often referred to as the Pearl of the South, Ponce is the most populous city in Puerto Rico outside San Juan. Since my wife was in charge of this trek, I happily went where she wanted to go. The Castillo de Serrales, Plaza Las Delicias, which had the Lion's Fountain, Ponce Cathedral, and Parque de Bombas (old firehouse) were all on the events list. This is the city where the Don Q rum is distilled. I had to throw that in here. After going to these places, taking many pictures, and taking a stroll and browsing through the many different shops, it was time to lunch. We saw Lola Restaurant, which was at the center of the city. The atmosphere was nice; artwork by a local artist was on the walls, and the décor was contemporary, colorful, and vibrant. Since it was in the middle of the day, there were not many customers. I fell in love with this place. The complimentary bread with balsamic vinegar started off the food festivities. Soon to follow were *bolitas de maduro* (plantain balls mixed with chorizo); criollo trio, which came with mini codfish fritters, alcapurrias, and fried cheese; and seviche made of mahimahi and fried plantains. Since we had a good serving of appetizers, my wife and I decided to share a main course. Mofongo is one of the national dishes in Puerto Rico, but the waiter said that the mofongo served at their restaurant was something special. He was right. The cassava mofongo was very special. The cassava that the plantain was mixed with made it have a softer texture, almost like lumpy mashed potatoes but so much better. The garlicky flavor was easily noticeable, and the sautéed garlic cilantro jumbo shrimp that was laid on top, inside, and carefully laid around the mound of cassava mofongo made the dish ever more special. I fell in love with this dish. I have had mofongo in the past, but this

Lola Criolla dish is placed among my all-time favorite dishes. I could not stop saying how delicious, how unique, and how savory this dish tasted. Again, one of my all-time favorites.

After our time in Ponce had ended, we drove back north to the city of San Juan. While there, I worked on my tan. I was not sitting out on the beach or poolside or in the city at a nice park. We parked the car and walked around looking at the sites. I acquired the worst farmer's tan ever. But I do admit it was well worth it. San Juan is full of history. The five-hundred-year-old Castillo San Felipe del Morro stands on a hill looking ever so impressive over the Caribbean Sea. The Catedral de San Juan was built in 1540 and is a must-see in the city, as well as El Yunque, El Fortaleza, and many more attractions. This is also a port city, so you saw cruise ships docked and its passengers wandering all around the city. After a day of walking and being out in the sun for most of the day, we were tired. Since we were only going to be in San Juan for one day, rather than going out to dinner, we decided to just stay in for the evening and eat in the lounge area and take advantage of the free tapas that were being served. Hotel points definitely paid off during this trip. Mini mofongo with beef, jicama salad with cranberries, a variety of cheeses, wine, and so much more were offered in the lounge. My wife had her fill and decided to take our son out to the beach. I stayed in the lounge area and had several servings of the tapas along with Medalla beer and wine to finish my meal off. I felt like a king in that lounge binging on Puerto Rico's cuisine. I was in food heaven.

Unforgettable. That is how I would describe both my trips to Puerto Rico. As I mentioned earlier, the people and food of the island were what stood out the most. Puerto Ricans are beautiful people. Other than beauty in their physical features, they are very nice. The hospitality we received during both visits has yet to be surpassed. The food was out of this world. I felt like I was eating food from the motherland. The cuisine was savory, hearty, and so comforting. I gained weight during both trips to Puerto Rico, and every pound gained was so worth it!

Beef Nilaga (Filipino Beef Stew)
Yield: Serves 5

Ingredients

3 lb. beef chuck, round, and/or beef brisket cut into 2-in. chunks

6 c. water *[more or less water may be needed depending on stock pot size]

1 yellow onion, medium, cut into 1-in. slices

1 1/2 tsp. whole black peppercorn

3 carrot, medium, peeled, 1-in. bias slice

3 celery with leaves, cleaned, 1-inch bias slice

1 c. green beans, fresh, cleaned

2 potatoes, peeled, cut into 1-in. chunks

3 tbsp. fish sauce **[add more fish sauce if needed]

2 c. white cabbage, Napa cabbage, and/or bok choy, chopped (3 in.)

Procedure

1. Place stockpot on medium-high heat. Add beef chunks and enough water so waterline is just above the beef, about six cups[*].
2. Cook for thirty minutes or until water is at a hard boil. During this braising process, check the beef periodically. Beef will release its impurities (called scum in culinary terms). Use a slotted spoon, remove and discard the impurities (called skimming the scum in culinary terms). This allows for a cleaner soup base at the end.
3. Once you have obtained a hard boil and removed all the impurities that you possibly can, lower the heat to medium and add onions and black peppercorns. Allow to continue to cook for 5 minutes.
4. Add carrots, celery, green beans, and add 1 tablespoon of fish sauce. Allow to continue to cook for 10 minutes.
5. Add the potatoes and 1 tablespoon of fish sauce. Gently stir and continue to cook until beef and all vegetables are tender, about 5–7 minutes.
6. Lower heat to simmer; add choice of cabbage or all three. Continue to simmer for 5–7 minutes.
7. Taste. Add more fish sauce if necessary[**].
8. Place in serving bowls. Serve with rice.
9. Enjoy!

Pancit Bihon Guisado

Yield: 15–20 servings

Ingredients

3 lb. bihon noodles (rice noodles)
2 lb. chicken thighs (boneless, skinless)
2 bay leaves
1 tbsp. black pepper
1 tbsp. garlic powder
1 tbsp. kosher salt
2 tbsp. vegetable oil
1 c. carrots, cleaned, halved lengthwise, cut on a bias
1 c. green beans, ends cut, sliced on a 1-in. bias
1 c. celery with leaves, halved lengthwise, cut on a 1/2-in. bias
1/2 head green cabbage, large dice
2 tbsp. garlic, minced
1 onion, medium, medium dice
1 c. snow peas or pea pods
1/2 c. lemon juice
2 c. soy sauce
6–8 c. water
20 lemon wedges (garnish)

Procedure

1. Turn stove to medium-high heat. Place chicken and bay leaves in a medium stockpot; add water. Bring chicken to a boil then reduce to a simmer. Cook for 20–25 minutes.
2. Discard bay leaves; place cooked chicken thighs in a bowl, set aside, let cool to room temperature. Place chicken stock in a container; set aside for later use.
3. Once chicken has cooled, shred then set aside.
4. Open rice noodles package, place in a large bowl, and soak in cold water for about ten minutes. Once done, strain noodles, set aside.
5. Place a medium saute pan on medium-high heat. Heat oil then add onions and garlic. Saute for 3 minutes or until garlic turns light brown and onions are translucent. Add carrots and snow peas; stir well. Saute for 3–5 minutes.
6. Add green beans, cabbage, black pepper, garlic powder, kosher salt, cooked sliced chicken thighs, and 1/4 cup of soy sauce. Mix well, saute for another 3–5 minutes. MAKE SURE NOT TO

OVERCOOK VEGETABLES! Turn down the heat of stove; place vegetables in a container and pour reserved liquid with chicken stock; set aside.

7. Place a large saute pan, preferably a wok if you have one, on medium-high heat. Place reserved chicken stock mix and 1 cup of soy sauce in saute pan. Once heated, place rice noodles in pan and allow noodles to soak up seasoned stock; allow to soak for 5 minutes. If stock still exists after five minutes, strain noodles and place noodles back in saute pan.

8. Add cooked chicken and vegetable mix; turn heat down to medium. Mix well for 5–7 minutes.

9. Add 1/4 lemon juice, mix well; taste. Add more lemon juice if needed.

10. Turn heat off. Use remaining soy sauce, lemon juice, and lemon wedges for garnish.

11. Serve hot. Delicious by itself or with accompaniments. Enjoy!

Phontastic Beef Noodle Soup (Big Pot)
Yield: 20–25 servings

Ingredients

4 3 in. pieces of ginger, fresh cut in half (lengthwise)
6 onions, peeled, halved
16 qt. water
3.5 lb. beef marrow or knucklebones
10 lb. beef chuck
5 lb. beef sirloin
10 green onions or scallions, sliced in half
1.5 c. fish sauce
1/2 c. brown sugar
1 tbsp. whole pepper corns
25 star anise
20 cloves
3 cinnamon sticks
2 tbsp. fennel seeds
2 tbsp. coriander seeds
3 tbsp. kosher salt
4 lb. bahn pho rice noodles (prepare according to package instructions)
cheese cloth

Accompaniments

10 jalapeno peppers, fresh (sliced into rings)
4 bunch cilantro (rough chopped)
4 c. mung bean sprouts
2 c. Thai basil (individual leaves)
12 limes (sliced into wedges)

Procedure

1. Using a spoon, scrape off ginger's outer skin; clean onion and slice in half. Using long tongs, place each piece of ginger and onion directly over an open flame, such as a gas stove, and allow to blacken, turning slightly as each side blackens. If no open flame, place directly on electric burner, turning slightly as each side blackens. **(If you are hesitant of putting ginger and onion**

directly on your electric stove, lightly oil cleaned ginger and onion, place on a baking sheet, and place in oven on high heat until ginger and onion outer skin begins to char.) Rinse off blackened skin, place in bowl, and set aside.

2. Place beef bones, beef knucklebones, or marrow in a large stockpot; add enough water to cover bones. Bring water to a boil for 5 minutes. Pour contents in a colander and thoroughly clean stockpot. This is important: totally clean out pot; this helps to have a clean broth. Place bones back in stockpot and add 16 quarts of water. Turn heat to medium high.

3. Add beef chuck, beef sirloin, cleaned ginger and onion, scallions, fish sauce, kosher salt, and brown sugar. Bring to a boil then reduce heat to a medium low heat. Make sure to skim off any impurities and fat that floats to the surface. Allow to slowly boil for about 30 minutes.

4. Take out beef sirloin and half of the beef chuck chunks; leave the rest in with the stock. Place sirloin and beef chuck to an ice bath; this allows it to cool faster and stops the cooking process. Once cooled, wrap in plastic, place in refrigerator for later use.

5. Place star anise, cloves, cinnamon sticks, fennel seeds, coriander seeds, whole black pepper in a medium saute pan. Place on stove on medium heat and toast until fragrant, making sure not to burn (about 2 minutes). Remove from heat and allow to slightly cool. Using a cheesecloth, place dry ingredients in the center, grab all sides, and form a ball. Using a long piece of additional cheesecloth or kitchen string, tie up spices in cheesecloth. Place in broth.

6. Turn heat down to a low boil, allowing the broth to simmer for 4–6 hours. Make sure to periodically check the broth; skim and discard impurities and fat if floating on top.

    Adjust the seasoning as needed by adding more fish sauce or sugar if needed.

7. While broth slowly simmers, prepare accompaniments: slice jalapeno peppers, tear cilantro apart, separate Thai basil leaves, clean mung bean sprout, and slice lime in wedges. Place all in separate container; place in refrigerator for later use.

8. Prepare bahn pho rice noodles according to the package instructions. Prepare an ice bath for the noodles. Once noodles are cooked, place in ice to stop the cooking process. Drain noodles, place in container, and place in refrigerator for later use.

9. Take cooled beef sirloin and beef chuck out of refrigerator and place on cutting board surface. Slice each piece thin, separate while placing on serving plate. Refrigerate again for later use.

10. Prepare finished broth: Place a metal colander or strainer over another stockpot, making sure it sits on top of the pot. Turn off heat. Carefully take remaining beef chunk out of stockpot; place on cutting surface and shred into large pieces; set aside. Carefully pour stock over colander/strainer, allowing strainer to catch cheesecloth and bones. Pour enough of the stock for use during service. Transfer remaining stock to safe container; allow to cool down. Once cooled, cover with a lid or plastic wrap; place in refrigerator for later use.

Preparing a *Pho*ntastic Bowl

1. Place 1–2 cups of rice noodles in a bowl.
2. Place a few slices of medium rare beef slice over rice noodles.
3. Add 2 cups of beef stock, or just enough to cover rice noodles.
4. Place a few pieces of beef sirloin and shredded beef chucks on top.
5. Add accompaniments: mung bean sprouts, Thai basil, jalapeno slices, and a couple slices of lime on the side.
6. Eat, slurp broth, and enjoy!

Six

AMUSE-BOUCHE
MEMOIRS, IN THE USA

Our First Trip to the United States

To this very day, my parents still enjoy telling this story to their friends and our relatives. When I was younger, I would get so embarrassed by this story, but now I laugh away with those who have heard the story. It's not so much of an overwhelming, courageous, exciting story. It's just about a little boy wanting his milk to drink while he was falling asleep.

My mother was already in the USA working as a nurse in Southern California. My mother ventured off to the USA a couple of years before us so she could save up money for us to eventually move there with her. That time finally came, and we (dad, older brother, and I) packed our bags; and after a big send-off party given by our relatives, we were off to the Land of Opportunity. We boarded a Pan-American (Pan-Am for short) full of excitement and sadness at the same time. My dad says we were all excited because we were soon going to be with our mom, we were going to be living in the USA, and also because it was our first plane ride. He also claimed we were scared because it was our first plane ride. Sadness also loomed over our heads since we were leaving our relatives in the Philippines, especially our grandparents who cared for my brother and me after my mom left for the USA. We took off, and we were on our way.

As this story unfolds, my father claims that I started to become restless sometime during the flight. I mean, it is a total of twenty or so hours from the Philippines to California. What child doesn't become restless! I don't recall too much about the flight, so everything written up to this point is straight from my father's point of view. I do remember several things that have happened to me at the age of five, but for some reason, I just don't remember the plane ride. Restlessness soon fell upon me, and my dad only knew one way that I would settle down, keep quiet, and eventually fall asleep. My innocent-looking dad turned toward the flight attendant and motioned for her assistance. "What can I do for you, sir?" she asked. My dad responded with his best nonaccented voice, "Do you have a bottle?" "What kind of bottle do you need?" the flight attendant remarked. With a squeaky voice, my dad responded, "A baby bottle, please." Looking quite confused, the flight attendant looked at my dad and said, "Yes, we do have spare baby bottles, but where is the baby?" Being quite embarrassed already from the entire situation, my dad answered the flight attendant with the softest voice, "It's for him." And he pointed at me! Yes, everyone, I needed a baby bottle to keep quiet the rest of the long plane ride to the United States. I was five years old!

The Baby Bottle

From my understanding, I loved my baby bottle. I would have it with me wherever I went, which meant the front and back yard of my grandmother's house, the bedrooms, bathroom, kitchen, etc. If day trips were taken, a baby bottle was stashed in my mom's, aunt's, or nanny's purse. Yes, I loved my baby bottle. Now how I was able to break "the bottle" habit is quite amusing and unjust at the same time. My mom was concerned that I was too attached to this baby bottle that something had to be done. Keep in mind I was five years old, and most children stop drinking out of the bottle at two years old. She tried hiding it, throwing it away, or would just give me a cup to use, but I always wanted my bottle, especially when I slept. I definitely needed my bottle. But she did one last thing to eventually have me stop. She stated, "If you don't stop drinking out of the bottle, the policeman will come and get you." Now what kind of psychological nonsense was that! What kid at the age of five is not afraid of the policeman! Keep in mind it was just a couple of months since we arrived in the United States. It was a new land, new culture, and new policemen. I was not about to get taken away by "the man." That did the job, no more baby bottle. I wonder if this has anything to do me liking to drink bottled beer so much in the past…hmmm.

Very First Day of Our Beloved Educational System

It was a beautiful sunny day in Coronado, California. The birds were chirping, the weather could not have been more than seventy degrees at 7:00 a.m. I was dressed in my uniform: black pants, white shirt, black sweater, and black dress shoes. Today was my very first day of twelve years of education: kindergarten. Sacred Heart Catholic Elementary School was located just a few blocks from our house. Since this was my first day of school, like all parents, they walked me to school. I held my mom's hand the entire walk. Emotions were racing through my head during the entire walk. Would I like it? Would the kids be friendly? Would I have any friends? I was the new kid on the block and didn't know what to expect in this new environment.

After checking into the school office, the head nun (sister) escorted me and my parents to the classroom. My heart was racing at this moment. The excitement soon turned to fright, and I didn't let go of my mom's hand. We walked into the classroom, and all eyes were on me. I could feel the stares and hear the whispers. My smile turned into a frown, and I wanted to get out of there. The head nun introduced Sister Mary (there is always a Sister Mary in every Catholic school) to my parents, and they all exchanged pleasantries. She then leaned over and started to reach for my right hand. I saw what she was attempting to do, but I beat her to it. I quickly threw my right hand behind my waist and hid behind my mom. I felt a little safe behind her thinking she was going to protect me, but boy was I wrong. She slowly moved over to the side and started to let go of my left hand. My vise grip on her hand was slowly losing its strength, but I still managed to hold on. Sister Mary was able to gently grab my right hand and started to pull me toward her. This is when the fright totally came out, and my eyes filled with buckets of tears. My mom slowly let go of my left hand and started saying good-bye to the nuns and lastly to me. The last thing I remembered her saying was, "You will be fine, and I will see you soon." "Maaa, Maaa, Maaa, Maaa!" was all I could say. My parents slowly walked out of the classroom. The buckets of tears raced down my face, and I didn't care that every student was looking at me. I wanted my mom. Soon after, I was escorted to my desk while still weeping. The only desk available was situated close to a window. This brought a little hope to my mind. Rather than sitting on the chair, I stood next to the window and looked out for my mom. I saw a young couple about a block away from the school. I wanted to yell out, but no sound came out of my mouth. I was scared of all the strange kids in the room. I kept to myself and continued to look out the window. Sister Mary saw that I was scared and enticed me to sit by putting a matchbox car on my desk and rolling it back and forth. I didn't move. I was like a soldier working the front gate gazing out the window. She gave up, let me stand, but left the toy car on my desk. Since I didn't have too many toys at home, my soldier stare out the window slowly started to weaken. I started eyeing the toy car. My eyes were no longer moist, and the tears had dried up on my face. I slowly turned around and was soon playing with my new toy. I finally sat down but paid no mind to anyone in the room. This toy car was now my favorite toy.

After three weeks of being in class, being scared was no longer the issue. I had friends that I talked, laughed, and played with. There were also a few who I didn't like, but I stayed away from them. I talked and laughed so much that it became my favorite pastime when in school. With this being said, one day, an envelope was given to me from Sister Mary. She instructed me to give it to my parents and that they had to sign it and I was to give it back to her. Without hesitation, I followed her instructions and did what I was told. When I got home, I handed the envelope to my parents. It was a report card. It stated I was doing well, but what surprised my parents is the note Sister Mary wrote. It stated, "Rommel is doing well but is very talkative in class. He gets along well with the others but at times is disruptive while others are paying attention." I went from being the quietest to the noisiest, most talkative, in my first month of my educational career.

Spring Break, Daytona Beach

One year, for spring break, I headed down to Daytona Beach, Florida. I flew down there from Washington DC and met up with an old high school friend, Rob, and four of his college buddies from Oklahoma University. When I left DC, it was a cold day and I had on a thick sweater. I get to Florida, step out of the plane, and it is sixty-five degrees outside. Since I arrived in the evening and the party clock was ticking,

Prix Fixe: Made in the USA by a Filipino

I skipped the unpacking and kicked off my spring break immediately with a beer. We pregamed at the hotel for a while before heading out for a night of debauchery. The night started out with a bit of bar-hopping while we tried to find the right place. We ended up at a good club, but in no time, it filled up. It got too packed for us, so we headed out in search for the next bar. As I was walking out of the club, a pretty little thing caught my eye. I walked with her at a casual pace while flirting it up. Perhaps I got too caught up in her to realize that Rob and his friends were not with me anymore. I waited and looked around, but to no avail. Mind you, this was before the wonderful technology of cell phones was created, so I was at the mercy of my eyes and ears to find them. I went back inside the club and had a few more beers while wandering around and looking for my partners in crime. Alas, they were nowhere to be found. So I decided I might as well head back to the hotel, and maybe we would meet up there sometime before the end of the night. This decision was in haste, I realized. I had no clue how to get to the hotel; I didn't even know the name of it! You can imagine the mixed emotions I was feeling at that point. It is my first night in Daytona Beach, I am consumed with spring break fever, and I am alone, lost, and wearing a sweater during a warm Florida night. Well, that last part of the dilemma was easily solved. I removed my sweater, tied it around my waist, and began walking down the beach in what I thought could be the direction of our hotel. The fun thing about my predicament is that it was spring break, so the beach was just as crowded as the bars and the streets. There were people all around walking, partying and drinking. Thankfully too because the next thing I know, I hear a voice yell out to me, "You look lost!" I turned with a smile and mumbled something about heading to a bar. They told me I should I just hang out with them and have a few beers. The gentleman that I am, I obliged them. Over a few hours, I had a few beers with these fellow spring breakers from South Carolina and had a great time. That lonely, lost feeling I had when I was separated from my friends melted away rather quickly. Eventually, I decided it was time to continue my search for my friends, so I thanked my new friends for the beers, and I headed off down the main strip. It was 1:00 a.m., but there were still tons of spring breakers out on the street, so I was hopeful about finding my buddies. Shortly after getting on the street, I hear my name being yelled out and see Rob's head hanging out of a car driving by on the strip. I jumped in the car and found out that they had been searching for me for the past two hours. It was good to be missed. Throughout the week, we nourished ourselves with the food of any true college student on spring break: fast food and junk food. If we ate anything other than McDonald's, Burger King, chips, and cookies, I sure don't remember. Then again, if I remember a lot from that week, then it probably wasn't a good spring break. The week ended early for the college boys because they ran out of money toward the latter half of the week. Since they drove from Oklahoma, they needed to save the rest of their money for gas. Rob and I had enough money, but we didn't have enough for the rest of the crew. They decided they wanted to leave early. My flight was not until early the next day. I had no place to sleep. Rob had befriended a couple of girls from Wisconsin and had asked them if I could sleep in their room for the night. They were a bit hesitant, but with Rob's smooth moves, they agreed that I was a safe guy, and they allowed me to sleep in their room for the night. I left early the next day. What happened in the room with the two girls? Some things you just keep to yourself. What a great week in Daytona Beach!

The Wedding Adventure

Ken and I were invited to attend Donnie's wedding in Monterrey, California. It was a very special occasion not only for Donnie but also for Tony, one of our other friends. Both parties were unaware that their wedding day was scheduled on the same day. The invites were given out to us all to attend the ceremony, but we were not sure which to attend. We definitely could not be at two places at the same time. Tony and his beautiful wife were getting married in Chicago, and Donnie's wedding was on the west coast. For those of us who could attend the ceremony, we agreed we would split up. So Ken and I were going to Monterrey while my older brother, Roland, and Don were going to attend Tony's wedding.

Our adventure began in the smoke room of *Chateau Mendoza* the night before our departure date. Now this is what I called my house due to…well, it was just a good house name. The smoke room, well, we smoked (cigarettes, ahem) in there, ha ha! Anyways, we spoke about our trip, friends we were going to meet, and finally drove down from San Francisco to Monterrey to attend the wedding. We were hyped, we were ready.

We left quite early the next morning. I had pissed off my dad on the way to the airport, so it was a quick good-bye at the curbside and off he went. While checking in, I could not find my driver's license to show verification. I was at a loss. I was already booked on the next flight out, which was two hours after my original flight. This gave me enough time to go home and find my ID. Rather than calling my dad to come get me, I decided to take a taxi home to find my ID. After ten minutes of looking for it, I found it. Stupid me, I had placed it in the suitcase I was using. Yes, careless move, I know. Hell, I was excited to be headed to the "Weeest Siiide!"

Ken went on the original flight, and we were to meet at San Francisco International Airport. He had an old college friend who resided in Walnut Creek, California, who was going to pick us up. It was now a race to the west coast. Ken's plane had an emergency landing right after takeoff; it landed at Dulles International Airport. The flight attendants smelled smoke on the airplane…more about this later.

My flight was rather uneventful except for the fact that the old gentleman sitting two seats beside me had awful gas! If it wasn't coming out one end, he was burping it out. I held two fingers up my nose for the first hour of the flight. I usually do not get up during a flight, but the smell was overwhelming. It smelled like a mixture of old wet socks and eggs. I excused myself from my row and walked ever so slowly to the bathroom. As I walked near the bathroom, one of the flight attendants looked at me with a sorrowful look on her face. She said that there were spare seats in the emergency row. She knew of and saw my pain. She then whispered, "When I walk by your row, I hold my breath." I am quite sure she saw me sitting with my two fingers up my nose; I probably looked like an ass! Anyways, what she said put a smile on my face. I thought I was the only individual smelling hell on this airplane! I moved to the spare seat in the emergency row and sat patiently as we headed to our connecting city, Dallas/Fort Worth International Airport. This was my first time landing in this airport. I had an hour and a half layover, so I figure I would tour this rather exciting airport. I bought some hot sauce, ate Texas BBQ, and finally found a Dallas Cowboys store. I am a *big* Cowboys fan, and I thought I was in football heaven;

Prix Fixe: Made in the USA by a Filipino

Dallas Cowboys gear and clothing everywhere! I even tried on the huge cowboy hat and big finger that you see jackasses on TV wearing. I finally boarded my flight, and I was on my way.

After a few hours, I landed safely in San Francisco and walked out of the arrival gate. This was pre-9/11, so I was anxious to see Ken and his college buddy meet me at my arrival gate. There was no one. I walked by an airport bar near the gate and only saw a couple of people in there. I walked down to baggage claim; no welcoming party. I got my bag, made a call to Ken's cell phone, but no answer. I went outside, smoked a cigarette, and started saying, "Where the hell are you!" After thirty minutes of waiting, I went to a customer service agent and asked if a "Ken Rogers had arrived?" Due to security purposes, she could not disclose that information to me, but she did inform me that there was a Rogers on a flight from Los Angeles. Los Angeles, I thought, that was not a layover city of the original flight. What were the chances that it was my friend who was on that flight?

I stepped back outside to think this scenario over. About fifteen minutes had passed, and after smoking two cigarettes, I realized that I was in a bind. I thought about calling my relatives in the area, but I was on an adventure; and having relatives rescue me was not an objective of mine. I paced back and forth, thinking of possible solutions. Several minutes later, I hear this loud "Rooommmel!" I looked, and it was Ken! He had a wild flight coming to the west coast. Ken's plane had an emergency landing right after takeoff. There was smoke on the plane; the pilot decided to make an emergency landing at Dulles International Airport. The gate agent at Dulles Airport informed him that he would be on the next flight out to San Francisco that departed three hours later. This was not a good enough solution for Ken. He then heard that a flight was boarding for Los Angeles. From Los Angeles, he would catch a connecting flight to San Francisco, arriving thirty minutes later than the original flight. Ken didn't hesitate; he was bound for Los Angeles.

I got introduced to his college buddy; Aron was his name. He looked very familiar. He looked at me and asked if I walked past a bar at the gate area. I said, "Yes, sure did." One of the individuals I saw at the airport bar near the gate of which I arrived was his college buddy. We all laughed! As we proceeded to walk to Aron's car, he handed us a "Welcome to California" gift. Aron then pretended he had a movie camera and said, "The movie has started."

It was close to happy hour; so rather than checking into our hotel, Aron wanted to take us to his local watering hole that he frequented during the week. The place was called Golden Bear and was located in downtown Oakland. The place was rather small inside but had a good feel to it. After ordering our drinks from the bar, we briefly sat on the bleachers that were situated next to the wall in front of the bar. It was rather interesting seeing bleachers in a bar. Our first drink soon turned into our third drink, and we decided to sit outside and enjoy the California sun. As soon as we walked out, I noticed one of the employees, a rather older gentleman, preparing some fish. Not just any ordinary fish—but catfish. He was preparing to deep-fry it. He had a propane burner, a large pot filled with hot oil, a warmer, plates, and tartar sauce for dipping—all situated just to the side of the front entrance to Golden Bear. To my amazement, he was set up for a fish fry outside in the city of Oakland. A fish fry in the middle of a city; this does not happen on a daily basis. I walked to the older gentleman in charge of the fish fry and exchanged greeting. I learned that he had lived in Oakland for over twenty years but was from the east coast, South Carolina to be exact. He saw me eyeing his fish and asked if I knew anything about deep-frying catfish. I was still a rookie in the culinary world, so I told him I didn't know much. To my surprise, he started to explain the necessary techniques on how to have a soft and flavorful fish while not overcooking the batter. Since he was originally from the South, he knew what he was talking about. Without hesitation, I ordered a fish basket that consisted of two large pieces of fried catfish, french fries, and homemade coleslaw. After receiving my order, I sat in the designated seating area and took a bite of the fish. It was absolutely delicious. As he stated, the fish was soft and flavorful with a hint of spice to it. The batter was not overwhelming. There was just enough batter to hold the fish in place; a good ratio of fish and batter. The homemade coleslaw tasted fresh with just enough lime juice and sugar to balance out the flavor. I was in fish-fry heaven. As soon as I finished eating, I walked back over to the older gentleman, looked at him in the eyes, and said, "You are the master of the fish fry." I shook his hand and thanked him. He then told me to remember the key to a successful fish fry. Aron soon commented that this is what they do during happy hour. I will never forget Golden Bear, but most importantly, I will never forget the fish-fry man. Now this is just the beginning of this adventure, but I will leave it here for now. This story is to be continued.

Maya Mango

Yield: 2–3 servings

Ingredients

2 c. mango, fresh, medium chunks
1 c. pineapple, canned
10 ice cubes
1 c. pineapple juice
1 tsp, kosher salt
2 tbsp. honey

Procedure

1. Place all ingredients in a blender; cover.
2. Blend until smooth.
3. If a sweeter taste is desired, add juice from the canned pineapple.
4. Enjoy!

Pear of Sunsets

Yield: 2–3 servings

Ingredients

2 c. Asian pears, cleaned, skin on
1 c. Bosc pear, cleaned, skin on
1/4 c. pineapple, canned
10 ice cubes
1/4 c. lime juice
1/2 c. pineapple juice
1/4 c. heavy cream
2 tbsp. honey

Procedure

1. Wash and clean all fruits.
2. Place all ingredients in a blender; cover.
3. Blend until smooth.
4. If a sweeter taste is desired, add juice from the canned pineapple.
5. Enjoy!

Seven

The Past

As I sit here thinking about my culinary world, I have come to realize that I have worked just about every back of the house position that exists in the culinary industry. For those who may not know what the back of the house means; it is the staff area where the cooks and other support staff works. This area is generally where food is stored, prepared, and at times consumed in the break room by staff while on break. Cooks, expediters, and dishwashers work in this sometimes cramp area that is often unseen by the general public, unless the establishment has a glass wall so the customers of the establishment can view the kitchen while in operation. Anyways, a breakdown of the position I have held and continue to have:

fast-food employee
dishwasher
busboy
waiter/server (I consider this position both front and back of the house)
prep
prep cook
assistant kitchen manager
sous chef
personal chef
caterer
business owner
executive chef
corporate executive chef

Rommel Mendoza

entrepreneur
husband
father
dreamer

Working at Burger King at Patrick Henry Village in Heidelberg, Germany, was my very first job in the food service industry. Before starting employment at Burger King, new hires had to attend an all-day (six hours) orientation. My best friend, Ken, and I got hired the same time and scheduled to attend orientation the same day. Ummm, that was something that they should have never done. Before taking the bus to the orientation site, just like your average teenagers who had little direction, Ken and I decided to partake in some flavored beverages. The bus finally arrived, and off we went feeling like the weekend had started...in our thoughts.

During orientation class, we would not make eye contact. Our names were called out to answer questions, but blank stares and incorrect answers were the norm. We giggled like little boys during summer camp. And this went on for six hours! By the end of the orientation class, our buzz was gone, eyes were tired, and we were starving. We were given our schedules; we were to report to Burger King the next day.

Ken and I were both scheduled to work from 4:00 p.m. to 9:00 p.m. on our first day. I was fortunate enough to train on expediting food—in other words, working the front line, putting the order together and handing it over to the customer. Ken was not as fortunate; they trained him on the broiler: placing frozen burger patties on the conveyor that was about 500 degrees. On a hot day, you could easily lose weight while working this station. Throughout the five hours of working on our first day, I would so often look at Ken with a smile on my face. He acknowledged my smile and returned it with his own smile—his middle finger.

Other than working the various stations of Burger King (whopper/burger bar, chicken bar, broiler, etc.) ten little-known things would happen or have happened while working at this fine establishment.

1. We would play hockey in the back room using squeegees or mops as hockey sticks and an over-ripe tomato as the puck.
2. If you had friends working the other two food bars, personal orders would be taken, a signal would then be given, personal orders would be stashed in the trash, one person would take the trash out; we would then all meet outside, next to the trash bin, pull out our covered sandwich of choice, and have a silent snack outside.
3. If you had a hangover, a quick catnap in the walk-in was so inviting; it was also the best way to relieve the feeling of throwing up.
4. For some reason, it was always cool for someone to throw ice into the deep fryer. I did say someone; it was never me. You know who you are!
5. The Burger King uniform back then, during, the late 1980s, made the female employees' butts look really good; well most of them!

6. I remember sitting in Burger King for over four hours laughing with a good friend. For those who lived in Heidelberg, think about why anyone would sit in Burger for hours, laughing.

7. I got caught eating one evening while working the chicken sandwich bar. The manager at the time gave me a warning. I was such a rebel.

8. When the manager was not in house, an employee would get on the drive-through microphone and start rapping. Back then the Fat Boys collaborated with the Beach Boys and "Wipe Out" was often sung over the intercom!

9. *Everyone* who ever waited for their order was "hooked up" at least one time.

10. I would have never known that I would end up in the food service industry later in life. Thank you, Burger King, for all the memories.

I remember working as a busboy/dishwasher/waiter early in my early twenties. I didn't really understand the importance of these three positions back then. Come on, most people in their early twenties were just getting accustomed to going to bars, partying, and having a good time. Granted, I did attend college during this time, but that part of my life is another story. In my opinion, dishwashers, busboys, and waiters are the most underappreciated positions in the food service industry. Just imagine having half-eaten food dumped into your hands, or scraping leftovers off plates, or even having your hands burned due to hot pans being left on the side of the sink and no one warning you about it. It happens. After banquets or parties, dishwashers would have to stay later to make sure everything is clean, waitstaff must assist with cleaning the front of the house, busboys assist with cleaning the front and back of the house before ever leaving. Many customers do not realize this, but other than seeing a busboy pick up dirty dishes from a table; a server providing you with great service; and a dishwasher washing pans, pots, and dishes, there is more to their responsibilities than the general public will ever know. I have only listed a few of the many responsibilities of these three positions, and believe me there are more. I think I just want you all to realize that when you see a dishwasher walk out in the dining room to get a drink of water or take a breather, a busboy picking up dirty dishes and cleaning a table, or a waiter standing and waiting to serve someone, all I ask is to be kind and say hello and thank-you. It took me twenty years to realize that these three positions are the backbone of any food service establishment. My brother and I were fortunate to land jobs as busboys at the Officer's Club in Fort Belvoir, Virginia. This was our first job after coming back to the United States after living overseas.

Present Day

Let's fast-forward to present day. I am currently employed with a prestigious food service/hospitality company. I have been employed with Thompson Hospitality for six years, and I must say that I have the best job in the world! I was one candidate out of twenty-five who responded to an ad that was posted on Craigslist. I did some research on this company and was quite amazed by what the company had accomplished and its vision for the future. Out of the twenty-five, two were called for the second interview. I went in to my interview confident, but scared at the same time. I made sure to arrive early; I went over any possible answers that they may ask, and prepared myself. I was eager.

Six years later, I am now one of the corporate executive chefs for Thompson Hospitality. I overlook four retail brands that conduct business in the corporate, educational, healthcare dining world and also perform chef tables. Chef tables consist of entertaining corporate customers/employees. In this situation, you are a guest chef and cook cuisine that *wows* the crowd. I enjoy doing this but also love my responsibility of overlooking brands in the corporate, educational, and healthcare dining world.

During the six years that I have been with Thompson Hospitality, I have traveled to many places. Whether it's opening a retail brand in a hospital, a university, or a corporate building or entertaining patrons during a chef table, I have been everywhere! With this being said, rather than naming all the locations I have been to, I have broken down my travels to different regions and the cuisines I have enjoyed most.

The Northeast Region

I lived in Winchester and Wakefield, Massachusetts, from fifth to eighth grade. Imagine a Filipino kid speaking with a slight Boston accent. By all means, this is no disrespect to my friends living in that area. The accent will, at times, come out; and I still cheer for the Bruins! This area is also the first place I have eaten Maine "lawbsta" and went flounder fishing outside the Boston "hawba."

I have worked in New York City: American Express Corporate Building on Vesey Street; Goldman Sachs; Ernst &Young; and many Johnson&Johnson units in the New Jersey area, Connecticut, Rhode Island, Pennsylvania, Maryland, and Virginia. From the famous New York–style pizza and Katz's Deli to Tony Luke's Philly cheesesteak, seafood in Boston, the many diners in New Jersey, crab cakes from Maryland, and the famous Smithfield ham from Virginia—I have had it all! Other than the unique eats that each state brings to the table, the people in this region are a bit unique in their own way. The fast-paced hustle of the big cities in the Northeast Region is not to be seen anywhere else in the nation. They are in a race that never stops! It's a bit slower when you go below the Mason-Dixon line, but the hustle is still observed.

New York City

I remember the first time I went to New York City. I was in the fifth grade. My family, along with another family, drove down to New Jersey from Massachusetts. Once in New Jersey, we left our cars parked in a garage and took the subway to this famous city. The ride only took about fifteen minutes. The next thing I remember, I was walking out of a building, and there I stood between the Twin Towers. They looked powerful and majestic. I don't remember much about that trip, but the two giants will always be embedded in my mind.

Now as an adult, New York City is something different. It is a wild animal that never stops moving! Where are all the people going? I find myself always asking that question every time I am in the Big Apple. After one of many visits to this enormous, crazy, alive city, I was able to find my answer: they are going to work, going home from work, going to a party, going to the store, going to a friend's house, going to the park, they are going somewhere—I can go on about this unique and energized city, but if you have never been to New York City, you will have to go to experience what I am trying to explain here. I love New York! I admit it, I do.

Good Eats in NYC: Katz's Deli, 5th Avenue Deli, Ray's Pizza, several other pizzerias, hot dog stands on various corners

The Southeast Region

When thinking of the South, the first thing that comes to mind: Southern cooking. I know that some of you may be upset that I didn't mention the people, the BBQ, and the hospitality. Yes, they are all important, but you have read this book this far, so you must like what you have been reading! I have a thing, a crush of a sort, on good old Southern cooking, or what some folks call Soul Food. From the good folks in Louisiana and Georgia who I have met and fed me Southern cuisine, I say, "Thank you!" I look at Southern cuisine as a friend's mama's cooking. It is food that is so good, so comforting that you wish you get invited to stay for dinner every night. I love it all. From the gumbo, etouffee, corn bread, collards to the fried okra and pickles—it is all amazing! But one dish that sticks out, that I must always have when in the South: fried chicken and waffles. (I can already hear you laughing. You know who you are!) Like the pizza in New York City, there is something about the juicy, fried chicken in the South, made by a Southerner, that can't seem to be replicated anywhere else I have been.

The other love I have is also in the South—in the most southern state, in the most southern part of the state—Florida and Cuban Cuisine. I have tasted Cuban fare in other regions of the nation, but Cuban cuisine in southern Florida is above the rest. Ropa vieja, chuleta de kan kan, and bistek are all favorites. But it's the puerco frito with its supporting cast: black beans, yellow rice, and orange garlic sauce called criollo that truly takes the cake! Pork chunks are slow roasted and then fried to golden perfection. Just thinking about it is making my mouth water! The Havana Café is a must stop every single time I am in the West Palm Beach area or even within a two-hour driving distance. This establishment is worth the drive.

Texas and Louisiana

Louisiana. Etouffee, gumbo, cajun catfish, poboys, and of course Bourbon Street. I can write so much about this area, but just like other beautiful, crazy, cities out there, you have to experience it yourself just to understand what is written. In addition, some things are meant to be kept to oneself.

Texas. Texas holds a special place in my heart. It's only fitting that I mention Texas since I have studied Tex-Mex cuisine and have grown to love the food and the spices that come with it. I have never lived there but have frequented the area many times. The people, the cities, high school football, the food, and of course the Dallas Cowboys are what makes this place so special, so eclectic, so amazing. One may ask, "The Cowboys. Why?" Well, people either like the Cowboys or hate them. I happen to be a die-hard Dallas Cowboys fan—since 1978! Well, this is another topic, and I am sure many of you don't want to read about my adoration for America's team! I am aware that there are many places in Texas that have incredible Mexican and Tex-Mex cuisine. There is one place that I visited that left a mark in my culinary life: Fuel City Tacos. There is a small picnic area for sitting outside, the space where the food magic takes place is as big as a large walk-in closet, and it is located in a gas station food market. Fuel City Tacos is located in Dallas, Texas, in the Fuel City Gas Station and Car Wash. They are known for their tacos (barbacoa, beef and chicken fajita, and pastor) wrapped in your choice of corn or flour tortilla. A true taco is wrapped in two corn tortillas topped with onions and red or green salsa. Each style of taco has its own distinct taste, unlike some tacos that suffer from being mingled too much with the grease from the meats that are cooked. These tacos are hands down some of the *best* tacos I have ever tasted. I just drooled; my mouth is watering.

Another city that has become one of my favorites just after my first visit is Austin, Texas. As the slogan for the city goes, "Keep Austin Weird"; that slogan holds true for this fascinating city. Other than being home to the famous SXSW Music Festival, it is also home to the many live music venues throughout the city. Live music is always present in the city. Last but not least, Austin is also the food truck capital of the nation. Food trucks line the streets, are on corners, and even have food truck food courts. It is just amazing seeing the food truck nation alive in this city. Like the state, everything in Texas is bigger. The portions are served big in most places I have been. With big portions comes big hearts. Texans are some of the nicest and most honest people you will ever meet.

What you should eat while in Texas: BBQ, BBQ, BBQ! Also, Tex-Mex cuisine and the variety of salsas, hot sauce, and guacamole.

The West Siiide

Seattle. Experience Pike Place. Throwing fish, the random cadence, and the multiple types of Asian cuisine are to be witnessed at this famous establishment. I also went to the first ever Starbucks establishment. Other than the Asian cuisine at Pike Place, I also enjoyed JapaDog, which are various hot dogs with Asian flair.

California. For those who may not know me well, and that is probably many of you, California is a home away from home for me. I have lived in California in the past, I have visited this state more than any other state, and I have many friends and relatives who live throughout the state. I love everything about this state. I get excited and sentimental every time I talk about it or even listen to someone talking about California. Whether it's the north or the south, California will always be home to me.

Prix Fixe: Made in the USA by a Filipino

Rather than talking about the division of Northern and Southern California and not getting anyone upset about which I think is a better region, to keep the peace, I will explain the state as a whole
and my present experiences. As mentioned earlier in the book, I was able to spend a little bit of time
with the locals in the Oakland, San Francisco, Monterey area. This area is "hella" cool! That last sen-
tence was for you Northern Cali folks! The trees and the mountains are easily seen and enjoyed in this
area. Just like the south, people are friendly and laid-back. Chinatown in San Francisco is a must visit if
you are ever in this beautiful city. You would think that the food would taste the same in every Chinese
food establishment, but it sure does not. I had the same thought when visiting Texas for the first time.
I thought every Tex-Mex establishment would taste the same, offer the same food, and look the same.
I was completely wrong. Similar to Texas, Chinese food in Chinatown was eclectic, unique, and absolutely delicious! Just about every region of China is represented in Chinatown.

Another aspect of Northern California that I enjoyed and is a must-try is just north of San Francisco,
in wine country. There are too many wine vineyards to name, and I am sure each one offers a varietal
difference from the other. But driving along the hillside, seeing the vineyards, and of course tasting
the products is something to experience. Since I am a chef, the vineyard I had my first tasting was on
the house. It pays to be a chef! But most vineyards will charge between $30 and $100. This will depend
on what is included in your tasting. I suggest that if you go to a wine tasting and just go for the tasting
itself with no meal included, go with a full stomach. My first tasting, I went on an empty stomach. By
the fourth glass, I was friends with the manager, his assistant, and had a smile a mile wide. Oh, I could
have spitted out the wine I tasted, but why waste good wine!

Southern California, how I miss you so! When I mention SoCal from this moment on, I am refer-
ring to San Diego County. Yes, Los Angeles is part of Southern California, as well as its surrounding
cities; but to me, Los Angeles County is similar to New York City, just not as wild. The sun, the beach,
the people, and the laid-back attitude are what make this region one of my favorites. La Jolla, known as
the Jewel of California, is my favorite place. If I had a choice to live and retire, La Jolla would be that
place. I fell in love with that small city ever since I first stepped on the rocks that make up the coastline
and witnessed sea lions tanning on the shore; this was over twenty years ago. I also had my first Bloody
Mary with a crab claw as a garnish at one of the restaurants that overlooked the blue Pacific Ocean.
Back then, McDonald's had the McSnack; not quite a McDonald's but big enough to walk up, place an
order, and wait for your order while enjoying the weather outside. It never fails that every single time
I visit La Jolla, I end up lying down on the open grass field and just enjoy the gentle sea breeze, the
California sun caressing my face, and the sounds of the ocean and mankind intermingling with one
another. I would close my eyes and just absorb my little piece of heaven. Aside from La Jolla, my other
favorite places include Coronado, Point Loma, Pacific Beach, Ocean Beach, and Mission Bay.

When it comes to food, Mexican cuisine is a must! Yes, there is Tex-Mex in Texas, but to get the true
authentic taste of Mexico without having to go to Mexico, Southern California's Mexican food scene
is incredible. Maybe it's just me, but Mexican food cooked in Southern California tastes better than
anywhere I have been. You can taste the freshness and the authentic flavors that should come from

true Mexican food. To my Mexican friends out there, I am sure the cuisine produced at home tastes absolutely incredible. So where is my invite?

Real tacos are made and eaten with corn tortillas rather than flour tortillas. So many salsas; there is just too many to name. Rather than tasting the usual red or green salsas, explore the unique: eggplant, green apple, mango pomegranate, and many more.

Other than the great Mexican food that Southern California has to offer, the California burrito, (carne asada burrito with french fries), the abundant Filipino restaurants, fish tacos, and Hawaiian BBQ should all be on the list of Must Try. I can write an entire chapter on Hawaiian BBQ, but for now, there are a few choice foods I would like to mention: Loco Moco (consists of white rice, hamburger patty, brown gravy, and topped with fried egg), Kahlua Pig (roasted pig cooked in an underground oven called an imu), Korean short ribs, and musubi. One place I have visited a few times during my stay in SoCal is Island Style Café in Tierrasanta, California. It is a rather quaint little restaurant and well worth it. The employees are always smiling, and Hawaiian music is always playing. The food is out of this world! Come hungry because you will leave extremely satisfied. SoCal, I shall return—hopefully soon!

Sisig Recipe (Filipino Sizzling Pork)
Yield: 8–10 servings

For the Brine

2 lb. pig ears
2 lb. pork bellies
1 onion, large, cleaned, quartered
10 garlic cloves
2 green onion, rough chop
1/2 c. lemon grass, fresh, chopped
1/2 c. orange juice
8 c. cold water (enough to cover pig ears and pork belly)
1 tbsp. coarse black pepper
2 tbsp. kosher salt

Pork Sisig

2 lb. cooked pig ears, small dice
2 lb. cooked, grilled, pork bellies, small dice
3 tbsp. canola oil
1 onion, large, small dice
1/4 c. garlic, minced
1/2 c. green onion, thin slice
1/2 c. lemon grass, fresh, thin slice
1/4 c. jalapenos, fresh, deseeded, minced
1/2 c. rice vinegar
1/4 c. soy sauce
1/4 c. lemon juice, fresh
1/4 c. brown sugar
1 tbsp. coarse black pepper
2 tbsp. kosher salt
1 tsp. garlic powder
1/2 tsp. red pepper flakes
1/4 c. cilantro, chopped

Procedure

1. Turn stove to medium-high heat. Place pig ear, pork bellies, onion, garlic cloves, green onion, lemon grass, orange juice, and water in a large stockpot. Add 8–10 cups of cold water or until waterline is at least 2 inches above pork. Add kosher salt and coarse black pepper. Place on stove and cook for 30 minutes. Turn heat down to medium low and cook for an additional 30 minutes or until pork bellies are tender. Turn heat down to low; continue to cook pig ears for another 15 minutes.
2. Heat oven to 350 degrees. When pork bellies are tender, carefully take out of pot and place on large oven-proof casserole dish. Place in the oven; allow to roast for 30 minutes.
3. Pig ears will be tender! Using tongs and a large serving spoon, carefully take out pig ears from the pot, making sure not to break it apart, keeping the gelatinous skin from falling off the ears. The gelatinous, cooked, soft skin is what binds the end product together. Place on a flat container and set aside to cool. During the cooling process, the pig ears will harden a bit but will soften again during the sisig preparation. Discard the brine and the remaining contents.
4. Once pork bellies are roasted, carefully take out and place on a flat container; allow to cool. Any rendered fat from the pork bellies, place in a small container for later use.
5. Once cooled, cut the pig ears and pork bellies into small dice. Prepare all other ingredients.

Sisig Preparation

1. Heat a large saute pan to medium-high heat; add oil. Add onion and garlic, saute for 5 minutes.
2. Add lemon grass and jalapenos; saute for 2 minutes. Add prepared pig ears, pork bellies, rice vinegar, soy sauce, and lemon juice. Saute for 2 minutes
3. Add brown sugar, coarse black pepper, kosher salt, garlic powder, and red pepper flakes. Mix well. Turn heat down to medium and allow flavors to marry for 10 minutes. Stir at least 3 times during the 10 minutes. This will allow for pieces to char during the cooking process, which will give it that extra flavor.
4. Add more salt, pepper, garlic powder, red pepper flakes if needed.
5. Garnish with chopped cilantro. Serve with rice, baguette, crackers, by itself, and/or with beer!
6. Taste, share, and enjoy!

Eight

CARRYOUT...FOR NOW

I am currently sitting in my hotel room looking outside the window. The sun seems to be getting sleepy, but the white clouds still desire to dance. The vast Grand Prairie land engulfs the stores, hotels, and industrial buildings.

"Grand Prairie, where is that?" I can hear you asking.

Well, it is about a five-hour drive northwest from Edmonton, Alberta, on the Old Alaska Highway. I am in Grand Prairie to open yet another one of Thompson Hospitality's brands; Austin Grill Express is now in operation at Grand Prairie Regional College. Like all my openings, it has been well received. Never in my lifetime, I thought, Grand Prairie was a destination I would have encountered; but now I can add this city to my big list of cities I have been.

I have been very fortunate in my life. I was only five years old when we left the Philippines, and boy, I did not realize the adventure my life was going to give me. My parents paved the way for us to leave the Philippines. Their hard work led us to the Unites States, but it was their guidance, discipline, tradition, and unending love that was the light that steered me in the right direction. I would have never seen snow, felt the tropical Hawaiian breeze while drinking fresh coconut water. I would have never eaten real "lawbsta" from Boston, German schnitzel, rode on a gondola, and played in an international baseball tournament in a small town in France. I would have never eaten true French cuisine, seen Buckingham Palace, and even experience living in Germany while the beautiful country was still divided by the Wall. I would have never seen Korea, Japan, and even Mauritius. There are still so many "I would have never" moments I can mention, but it is my parents who have made it possible for me to have felt snow, lived in Hawaii, eaten "lawbsta" lived in divided Germany, and experienced many other places. This was only during the first thirty-five years of my life; there are more years and stories to follow. My parents are a part of my passion.

During the last ten years, the passion I have for food and the culinary industry is what brought me to many interesting places. My passion has allowed me to travel to many regions of the Unites States,

Canada, and back to France. I have met many interesting employees in the culinary industry as well as people out in the general public. From the best pizza in the world (yes, it's New York style) to the JapaDog in Seattle, the fish tacos in California, Southern cuisine, Cuban food in South Florida, Texas barbeque, and many more—I am very fortunate to have fed my soul, and stomach, with history and such incredible cuisine. How can I forget about Canada's specialty, poutine! I can write about the different cuisine that makes the United States so special, but I will save that for another time. I do admit that out of all the places I have been during my culinary travels, the best place will always be when I travel home. To me, it's like a present during Christmas, the feast during Thanksgiving, the happiness of Easter. I come home to a beautiful loving wife who continues to support me. My wife has made me a better man. I come home to my gifts, my sons. Their angelic smiles and warm hugs are their gifts to me; it always touches my heart. My family is part of my passion.

Passion is not only from the mind but also from the heart. So in other words, do something not because you have to do it, do it because you want to do it. Every place, every location I have been, an individual always says, "You are always smiling, why?" I always answer, "Because when you smile, someone will wonder why you are smiling. Also, it only takes seventeen muscles to smile as opposed to forty-three to frown. So why not smile more often, right!"

While working at a culinary corporate unit, an employee always asks, "Why are you so happy?" It's simple. "I have a hobby, not a job."

I am a Filipino, born in the Philippines, who has seen the world like no other. I hope you have learned a little about me as my journey in the culinary world and life continues on. I leave you *for now* with one of my favorite verses:

So, whether you eat or drink, or whatever you do, do all to the Glory of God. (Corinthians 10:31)

Longaniza Recipe (Patties)

Yield: About 36, 4 oz. patties

Ingredients

4.25 lb. ground pork
2.25 lb. ground pork fatback *(may substitute with bacon)
2 whole eggs, raw
2 tbsp. minced garlic
2 tbsp. minced jalapeno (deseeded)
1/2 c. rice vinegar
2 tbsp. soy sauce
1 c. brown sugar
1/2 tsp. ground ginger
1/4 c. kosher salt
1 tsp. ground black pepper
1/3 tbsp. ground oregano
1/3 tbsp. dried basil
2 tbsp. ground annatto seed powder
2 tsp. paprika

Procedure

*Fatback is the cut of pork taken off the back of a pig which contains very little to absolutely no meat or lean. You may have to go to a local butcher shop to purchase this since fatback is not sold in supermarkets. Some butchers in local markets may sell you the fatback.

You can also substitute fatback with thick sliced bacon. If you go this route, since bacon is presalted and cured, you will need to soak the bacon overnight in iced water to remove the excess salt. After soaking overnight, mince bacon until you have a texture of ground pork.

1. In a large bowl, place ground pork, pork fatback, eggs, minced garlic, minced jalapeno, rice vinegar, and soy sauce. Mix well.
2. Add remaining ingredients. Mix well.
3. After mixing thoroughly, place plastic wrap on top of mixture, making sure to completely press out all air bubbles. Tear off another piece of plastic wrap and cover bowl completely.
4. Place in refrigerator and marinate overnight.

5. Using a 1/4 cup measure, spray measuring cup with nonstick spray. Scoop a level measure of mixture into the measuring cup. Place measured mixture on a parchment-paper-lined baking sheet.

6. If needed, continue to spray the measuring cup and measure out mixture until done.

7. If you want bigger patties, follow the same steps but use 1/3 or 1/2 cup measuring cups; yields will be different.

To Store

1. Cut parchment paper into squares; large enough so a single patty can be placed on it.
2. Make sure to place a parchment paper square between patties.
3. Place in freezer bag and store in freezer until ready to cook.

To Cook

1. Depending on size of patties and saute pan, place 6–8 patties on saute pan. Add 1/4 of water and place on stove on medium-high heat.

2. During the cooking process, once water starts boiling, carefully turn patties over, lower heat to medium and continue to cook until brown on both sides. You will need to turn patties again to brown other side.

3. Continue to cook for another 5–7 minutes or until a food thermometer reaches 165 degrees. Patties will start to brown, sugar will start to burn with goodness; this is a good indication they are done.

4. Serve with rice, choice of egg. Enjoy!

Acknowledgment

I want to thank God first and foremost for making all things possible in my life; thank you for listening, keeping me strong during my weakest times, and keeping me safe during my travels. My wife Eva, God completed my life when we became one. I love our past and present adventures we have taken and look forward to making more beautiful chapters with you and our boys in our life story. My sons, Romeo and Raphael "Max", your smiles and laughter continue to keep me young at heart. My mom and dad, thank you for your magical moment which created me. Mom, you inspired my love for food; triggering my appetite to make sure everything I create taste good. Dad, thank you for opening my mind by taking us around the world and exposing me to me to different cultures. My older brother Roland who I shared an adventurous childhood; something I enjoy doing now with my own boys.

My HAHS family; even though our school has closed, the memories and "the glory of Heidelberg High" will always remain in our hearts and minds. Special thanks to those who shared their Eichbaum stories. Now the world knows how special 182 HauptStrasse 69112 Heidelberg, Germany was to many of us; thank you George and family.

My boss, Stephen Pierce, continues to believe in me and gives me support and faith. I thank you for all that you do. Warren Thompson (CEO of Thompson Hospitality) and Benita Thompson-Byas (Vice Chairman of Thompson Hospitality), thank you for not giving up on me. There was time when I thought leaving the company was the best decision. You both assisted in finding me a job after my last days with Thompson Hospitality. What company does that? Did I leave? Well, I am happy to say I am still employed with the best company! Thank you for giving me a sense of purpose in my position and all the praises given for all that I do. To my chef friends, Joint Venture colleagues, and my chef instructors at Stratford University, keep inspiring those around you because you all have certainly inspired me.

Last but not least, to all the food service employees out there; from the executive chef to the dishwasher; we are all one big family. Let's take care of one another.

Made in the USA
San Bernardino, CA
30 April 2019